His Holiness
Mahant Baba Ram Singh Ji Maharaj

गिआन अंजनु गुरि दीआ अगिआन अंधेर बिनासु ॥
gi-aan anjan gur dee-aa agi-aan anDhayr binaas.
The Guru has given the healing ointment of spiritual wisdom, and dispelled the darkness of ignorance.
हरि किरपा ते संत भेटिआ नानक मनि परगासु ॥१॥
har kirpaa tay sant bhayti-aa naanak man pargaas. ||1||
By the Lord's Grace, I have met the Saint;
O Nanak, my mind is enlightened. ||1||

AUTOMATE TO DOMINATE

4X Your Business Success with Cutting-Edge ***Profit*** Strategies and ***Stress-Free Operations***

AUTOMATE TO DOMINATE

4X Your Business Success with Cutting-Edge ***Profit*** Strategies and ***Stress-Free Operations***

PARAS BAMBHA

Worldwide Published by
Pendown Press

PENDOWN PRESS LLP

An ISO 9001 & ISO 14001 Certified Co.,

Regd. Office: 3767A, Kanhaiya Nagar,

Tri Nagar, Delhi-110035

Ph.: 8130886000, 9650072927

E-mail: info@pendownpress.com

Branch Office: 1A/2A, 20, Hari Sadan, Ansari Road,

Daryaganj, New Delhi-110002

Ph.: 011-45794768

Website: PendownPress.com

Edition: 2025

Price: ₹ 299

ISBN: 978-93-6338-626-6

Layout and Cover Designed by Pendown Graphics Team

Printed and Bound in India by Thomson Press India Ltd.

To all the entrepreneurs who dare to dream big and challenge the status quo. To those who are ready to break free from the ordinary and build something extraordinary. May your businesses contribute to the growth and prosperity of our nation, India.

TABLE OF CONTENTS

WHY I WROTE THIS BOOK

For years, I have seen my customers, suppliers, and fellow business owners struggle in the same way I once did—drowning in operations, constantly firefighting, and unable to scale. I often thought, *how much can I really share in a conversation?* That's when I decided to **compile everything I've learned into this book**—so that no SME owner has to go through the same painful trial and error that I did.

The strategies in this book are not **theoretical concepts**; they are hard-earned lessons from my own journey, built through **hits and trials, courses, workshops, books, and real-world implementation.**

The Gap This Book Fills

Most SME owners believe that **running a business means running operations.** This mindset is what holds them back from real success. The biggest gap in SME strategies today is the **lack of systems, automation, and structured delegation**—elements that separate struggling businesses from scalable ones.

This book is not just another business guide—it's **life-altering knowledge**. It's the **exact roadmap** I used to transform my own business, and it can do the same for any SME willing to embrace change.

How This Book Will Transform SMEs

The transformation lies in the **shift from operational dependency to system-driven success**. By implementing the frameworks in this book, SMEs will:

- **Reduce their daily operational burden** by automating repetitive tasks.
- **Scale without stress** by building a structured leadership team.
- **Boost profitability** through financial discipline and revenue allocation systems.
- **Gain clarity** on what truly matters—high-value growth activities rather than endless micromanagement.

What Makes This Book Different?

Unlike traditional business books that focus on broad theories, this book is **rooted in real-world application**. It offers:

- **Actionable frameworks:** Tested in real businesses, not just boardroom theories.
- **Step-by-step guides:** That SME owners can implement immediately.
- **A no-fluff approach**: Just practical strategies that work.

The Core Principles That Drive This Book

1. **Automation Over Effort**: The less time spent on manual tasks, the more time for strategic growth.
2. **Delegation Over Micromanagement**: A business should run on systems, not on the owner's presence.
3. **Profit Over Revenue**: Growth is meaningless without financial clarity and disciplined allocation.

4. **Scalability Over Survival**: A business that depends on the owner is a liability, not an asset.

Why You Should Listen to Me

I am not a coach, a consultant, or a self-proclaimed guru—I am **one of you**.

I founded **VLA Industries Limited** at the age of 21, immediately after completing my studies. VLA is a **farm machinery manufacturing company exporting to over 29 countries** and serving major clients like **Mahindra, Kirloskar, and many more**.

Today, VLA ranks **among the top 10 in India in several product categories**, but none of this came easy. Every success was built upon **multiple challenges, failures, trials, errors, and eventual breakthroughs.**

Most importantly, my business has grown **5-6X since implementing these strategies**—and it's still a work in progress. Growth never stops, but with the right systems, it becomes **structured, predictable, and stress-free**.

What You Will Gain From This Book

By implementing the strategies outlined in this book, you can expect to:

- **Free yourself from daily operations** and focus on growth.
- **Increase your profits** without working harder.
- **Create a leadership team** that takes ownership of key business functions.
- **Scale your business with confidence** without the fear of burnout.

If you take away only **one lesson** from this book, let it be this: **Your business should work for you, not the other way around.**

Your Next Step

Your journey to **automation, delegation, and exponential growth** starts now.

Take action today—visit **parasbambha.com** to stay updated, get exclusive insights, and continue your transformation towards a **stress-free, scalable business.**

Let's build something remarkable together.

CHAPTER - 1

The Golden Hour: *The Most Crucial Hour of Your Day*

Success in business isn't just about working harder; it's about working smarter. One of the most effective habits of high-achieving entrepreneurs is dedicating the first hour of their day to strategic thinking and planning. This "Golden Hour"—an hour before your employees arrive—is a game-changer that sets the right course for your business.

Why the Golden Hour Matters

Most entrepreneurs start their day responding to calls, emails, messages, and putting out fires. But reacting isn't leading. The Golden Hour allows you to take control of your day before distractions take control of you.

This hour is a sacred time for deep thinking, reflection, and planning. It's when you set the agenda rather than letting the agenda set you. It's about aligning your actions with your mission, vision, and business objectives.

The No-Distraction Rule

To make the most of your Golden Hour, eliminate all distractions. That means no phone, no laptop, no tablet—just you, a pen, and a notepad. This old-school approach helps you cut through the noise and focus on what truly matters.

Use this time to:

- Reflect on your long-term vision and mission
- Strategize your goals and high-impact tasks for the day
- Identify potential roadblocks and solutions
- Jot down fresh ideas and innovation opportunities
- Revisit your objectives and measure progress

How to Implement the Golden Hour

1. **Arrive an Hour Early**: Get to your office before the hustle and bustle begins. This gives you a peaceful environment to think without interruptions.
2. **Find a Quiet Space**: Choose a spot where you won't be disturbed. Your office, a private meeting room, or even a quiet coffee shop can work.

3. **Use Pen and Paper**: Writing by hand encourages deeper thought and better retention. It also minimizes digital distractions.
4. **Follow a Structure**: Spend the first 20 minutes reflecting on your long-term goals, the next 20 minutes planning the day ahead, and the final 20 minutes brainstorming improvements and innovations.
5. **Make It a Habit**: Consistency is key. The more you commit to the Golden Hour, the more powerful its impact will be on your business and mindset.

The Impact of the Golden Hour

Entrepreneurs who incorporate the Golden Hour into their routine experience increased clarity, better decision-making, and higher productivity. Instead of reacting to daily chaos, they proactively shape their business's direction.

The most successful leaders understand that strategic thinking is just as important as execution. The Golden Hour isn't just another productivity hack; it's a leadership discipline that separates thriving businesses from struggling ones.

CHAPTER - 2

Scheduling: *A Map of Your Time*

Success in business isn't about working more hours; it's about making the hours you have count. One of the most powerful yet underutilized tools for maximizing productivity is scheduling. As the saying goes,

"Either you run the day, or the day runs you."

The ability to control your time is what separates highly successful entrepreneurs, CEOs, and business leaders from those who constantly feel overwhelmed.

The Significance of Scheduling

Scheduling is more than just setting reminders; it is about creating a structured roadmap for your time. Without a clear plan, your day can easily be hijacked by distractions, low-priority tasks, and unexpected demands. When done correctly, scheduling ensures that you:

- Focus on high-impact activities that drive results
- Avoid getting caught up in non-essential tasks
- Maintain control and direction in your business decisions

Why Every Business Leader Swears by Scheduling

Every accomplished entrepreneur and leader follows a strict schedule. They don't leave their success to chance; they create a system that allows them to maximize their time and energy. By pre-planning your day, week, and month, you eliminate guesswork and ensure that every hour is spent purposefully.

Scheduling helps you:

- Prioritize tasks based on importance and urgency
- Allocate time for deep work without interruptions
- Prevent burnout by balancing work and personal life
- Develop discipline and consistency in daily operations
- Make strategic decisions with a clear and focused mind

Your time is your most valuable asset. How you spend your first hour and how you structure your day determine the success of your business. Implement the Golden Hour and a well-planned schedule, and watch how they transform your productivity, decision-making, and long-term growth.

Remember: *Success isn't about doing more — it's about doing what matters most.*

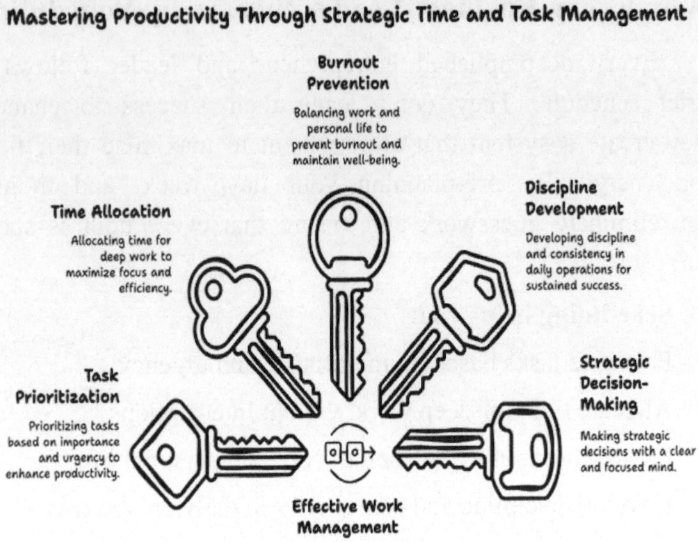

Choosing the Right Scheduling Medium

There is no one-size-fits-all method for scheduling. The key is to use whatever tool feels most natural and effective for you. Here are some popular options:

1. **Paper Planner or Diary**: Traditional yet effective, writing things down helps with memory retention and provides a visual representation of your day.
2. **Phone Calendar Apps**: Apps like Google Calendar, Apple Calendar, and Microsoft Outlook help keep everything digital and accessible across devices.
3. **Time-Blocking Techniques**: Allocating specific blocks of time for particular tasks helps minimize distractions and boosts efficiency.
4. **AI and Automation Tools**: Tools like Calendly, Todoist, and Notion help automate scheduling, reminders, and task management.

No matter which tool you choose, the key is consistency. Without scheduling, your day lacks direction—like a bullet without an aim.

How to Implement Effective Scheduling

1. **Start with a Weekly Plan**: At the beginning of each week, outline your top priorities and major tasks.
2. **Time-Block Your Day**: Allocate dedicated time slots for meetings, deep work, and breaks.
3. **Set Priorities**: Identify the top three tasks that must be accomplished each day.
4. **Avoid Overloading Your Schedule**: Leave buffer time for unexpected tasks and contingencies.
5. **Review and Adjust**: At the end of the day, reflect on what worked and tweak your schedule accordingly.

The Impact of Scheduling

Entrepreneurs who master scheduling experience increased productivity, better work-life balance, and a sense of control over their business. It transforms the chaotic hustle into a structured system, making execution seamless and efficient.

By treating time as your most valuable asset and using scheduling as a roadmap, you ensure that every minute contributes to your long-term goals.

CHAPTER - 3

The Power of Deep Work: *Unlocking Your Full Potential*

The Importance of Deep Work

In a world flooded with constant notifications, emails, and distractions, the ability to focus deeply on meaningful work has become a rare and valuable skill. Deep work, a concept popularized by productivity expert Cal Newport, refers to the ability to engage in high-concentration, distraction-free tasks that yield significant results. All successful businesses are the sheer result of constant deep work—focused effort over extended periods leads to groundbreaking innovations, powerful decision-making, and long-term success.

Entrepreneurs who master deep work are able to:

- **Solve Complex Problems:** Deep thinking allows you to approach challenges with clarity and efficiency.
- **Develop Innovative Strategies:** A distraction-free mind fosters **creativity and unique business solutions**.
- **Gain a Competitive Edge:** Those who can focus deeply will outperform those constantly distracted.
- **Increase Productivity While Reducing Burnout:** Concentrated work minimizes fatigue and enhances efficiency.

In today's **attention economy**, deep work is not just a productivity hack—it's a **superpower** that separates high achievers from the overwhelmed.

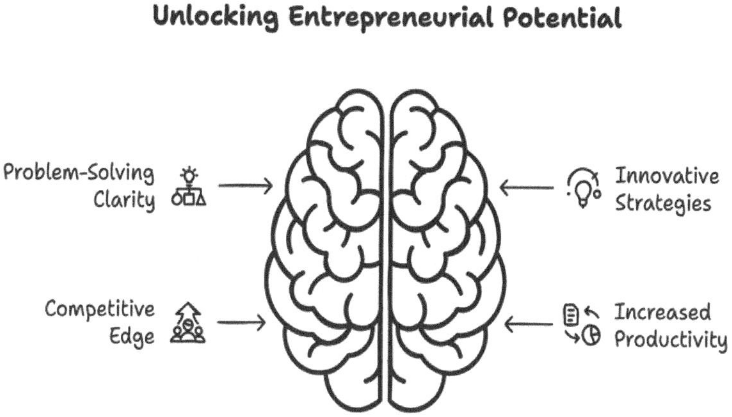

The Enemy of Deep Work: Digital Distractions

The modern entrepreneur's greatest enemy is the endless stream of notifications, messages, and social media updates. Social media apps, while marketed as tools for connection and information, often serve as black holes that consume valuable time and drain mental energy. Overstimulation from constant digital input weakens the brain's ability to focus, leading to shorter attention spans, decreased cognitive ability, and a struggle to concentrate on high-value tasks.

These distractions not only waste time but also degrade the quality of work. Studies show that constant digital interruptions can take up to 25 minutes to refocus on a task after being distracted. Imagine the cumulative damage this does over weeks, months, and years.

The Brain-Rotting Effect of Social Media

Social media apps are designed to keep users engaged for as long as possible, using dopamine-driven feedback loops that reward endless scrolling. For entrepreneurs, this addiction to instant gratification weakens the brain's ability to engage in deep, strategic thinking. The result? A foggy mind, constant mental fatigue, and a gradual loss of the ability to engage in deep work.

Unchecked social media usage:

- Shrinks your attention span and hinders decision-making
- Creates mental clutter that prevents clear strategic thinking
- Drains creativity and problem-solving capabilities

Steals time from high-impact business activities, reducing overall productivity and efficiency

Attention span decline hinders decision-making and creativity.

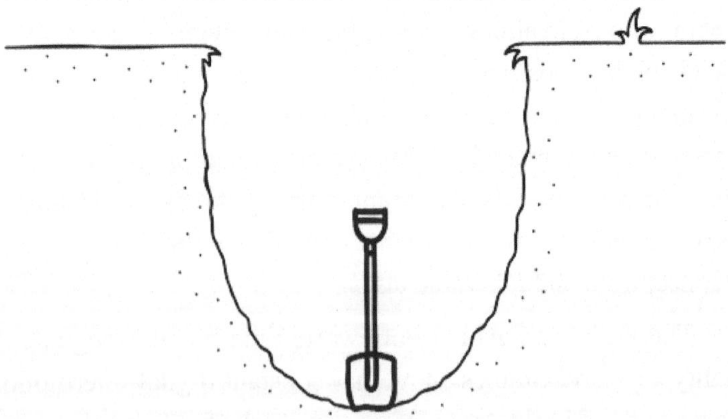

How to Regain Your Focus and Achieve Deep Work

If you want to harness the full power of your brain and maximize productivity, you must take deliberate steps to eliminate distractions and create an environment conducive to deep work.

1. **Delete Social Media Apps for a Few Weeks**: Experiment with removing social media from your phone for a set period. Most people find they don't miss it as much as they thought they would, and their focus significantly improves.
2. **Turn Off Notifications:** Disable notifications from messaging apps, emails, and social media to avoid constant interruptions. Each distraction resets your focus, making it harder to engage in meaningful work.
3. **Set Deep Work Sessions**: Schedule uninterrupted work blocks of 60-90 minutes where you focus solely on a single high-impact task. Protect these sessions like important meetings—no emails, no calls, no distractions.
4. **Use the Pomodoro Technique**: Work in focused sprints of 25-45 minutes, followed by short breaks, to maintain concentration. This method helps sustain mental energy and prevents burnout.
5. **Create a Distraction-Free Workspace:** Remove unnecessary gadgets, use noise-canceling headphones, and ensure your workspace promotes deep thinking. A clutter-free environment leads to a clutter-free mind.
6. **Engage in Analog Thinking:** Just like the Golden Hour, use a pen and paper to brainstorm ideas, write strategies, and map out your business vision without digital interference. This tactile approach fosters deeper insights and creative breakthroughs.

The Results of Practicing Deep Work

When entrepreneurs commit to deep work, they notice immediate and transformative results:

- Faster decision-making with greater confidence
- Increased efficiency and higher output in shorter time periods
- The ability to tackle complex challenges with ease
- A sense of clarity, purpose, and control over their business

Deep work is a superpower in today's distracted world. Those who master it gain a significant advantage over competitors who are constantly battling digital interruptions. If you truly want to 4X your business success, mastering deep work is non-negotiable.

CHAPTER - 4

Hire an Executive Assistant: *Your De-Facto CEO*

The Most Important Hire You'll Ever Make

One of the most significant steps in automating your business processes is hiring an Executive Assistant (EA). Your EA is not just an assistant—they are your **de-facto CEO**, the cornerstone of your second line of leadership. A skilled EA acts as the bridge between you and the operational demands of your business, allowing you to focus on high-value, strategic decisions rather than day-to-day management.

The Art of Delegation: From Small Tasks to Big Responsibilities

Most entrepreneurs struggle with delegation, but mastering this skill is the key to building a scalable business. Effective delegation isn't about offloading work—it's about empowering others to take ownership, freeing you to focus on growth and strategy. The process begins by systematically transferring responsibilities to your EA. Here's how to do it effectively:

1. **The First 30 Days: Daily 30-Minute Meetings**
    - Spend 30 minutes each day with your EA for the first 30 days.

- Use this time to hand over small administrative tasks like email management, scheduling, and minor decision-making.
- This builds trust and ensures that your EA understands your work style and business needs.

2. **Expanding Responsibilities Over Time**
   - Gradually assign larger, more strategic tasks.
   - Empower your EA to make decisions on your behalf.
   - By the 6-month mark, your EA should handle a significant portion of your workload with minimal supervision.
3. **Within 9-12 Months: A Fully Operational EA**
   - Your EA should now be capable of running the business in your absence.
   - They will anticipate problems, make executive decisions, and ensure operations run smoothly without constant input from you.
   - This transition allows you to shift your focus toward big-picture goals, expansion, and innovation.

The EA's Role: The Gatekeeper of Your Time and Business

Your EA is more than just a high-level assistant. Their role includes:

➢ **Managing Your Schedule:** They ensure your calendar reflects your highest priorities.

➢ **Filtering Communications:** They handle emails, calls, and requests, ensuring you only deal with what truly matters.

➢ **Coordinating Teams:** They act as the link between you and your leadership team, ensuring your vision is executed.

- **Decision-Making Authority:** Over time, they will take on key decision-making responsibilities, reducing your operational burden.

Location Matters: Why Your EA Should Be Office-Based

Your EA's efficiency comes from being **stationed outside your office** at all times. Unlike a personal assistant who follows you everywhere, your EA must remain in the office to:

- Ensure consistency and availability for your team.
- Keep operations running smoothly while you focus on higher-level strategy.

Manage all business communications and decision-making from a centralized location.

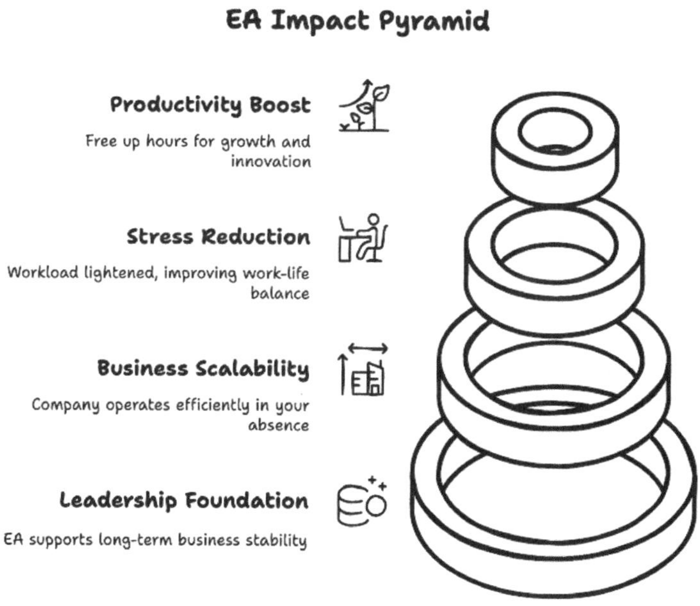

Aligning Your EA's Work with Your Own

Both you and your EA must be aligned in understanding what drives your business forward. Your main work is **profits, vision and strategy**, while your EA's work is **execution and operational efficiency**. This synergy ensures:

- **Seamless delegation** of tasks that don't require your direct involvement.
- **Faster execution** of business operations.
- **Increased efficiency** in decision-making and problem-solving.

Why Hiring an EA Is a Game-Changer

Entrepreneurs who hire an EA experience:

- **Increased Productivity:** You free up hours daily to focus on growth and innovation.
- **Reduced Stress:** Your workload is significantly lightened, improving work-life balance.
- **Business Scalability:** Your company operates efficiently even in your absence.
- **Stronger Leadership:** Your EA becomes the foundation of your second line of leadership, ensuring long-term business stability.

Final Thought: Your EA is Your First Step Toward True Automation

If you're serious about automating your business and multiplying your success, hiring an EA is the first and most crucial step. A well-trained doesn't just manage tasks—they become the backbone of your operations, allowing you to focus on high-impact decisions while they handle the rest. Commit to this process, and within a year, you'll witness a profound transformation—a business that thrives independently, scales effortlessly, and operates with precision, even in your absence.

CHAPTER - 5

Your Time is the Most Expensive Resource

Understanding the True Value of Your Time

As an entrepreneur, your most expensive and limited resource isn't money—it's time. Unlike money, which you can earn, invest, and multiply, time is finite. Once lost, it's gone forever. The way you choose to invest your time determines the trajectory of your business and personal success.

Calculating Your Money Value of Time (MVT)

To gain a clear understanding of how valuable your time is, calculate your Money Value of Time (MVT) using this simple formula:

MVT = Yearly Profit or Revenue ÷ 2,300

Why 2,300? Because that's the approximate number of working hours in a year for high-performing entrepreneurs. This number accounts for focused, high-value work time.

For example: If your business generates ₹1,00,00,000 in annual revenue, your MVT is ₹4350 per hour.

Now, every time you waste an hour on unnecessary tasks, extended phone calls, social media, or gossip, ask yourself: Would I willingly throw away ₹4350 (or whatever your MVT is) every time I get distracted? If the answer is no, it's time to make better choices.

RTI: Return on Time Invested

Once you've determined your MVT, evaluate how much time you're wasting on low-value tasks. This is where Return on Time Invested (RTI) comes in. Every hour you spend should have a tangible return that aligns with your business growth.

Some of the biggest time-wasters include:

- **Coordinating and booking tickets** instead of delegating to an assistant.
- **Unnecessary follow-ups** instead of using automated workflows.
- **Giving and assigning tasks manually** instead of using project management tools.
- **Extended conversations with employees** instead of structured, time-bound meetings.
- **Scrolling on social media or watching videos** with no business-related ROI.

Now, let's do the math—if you waste just two hours a day on non-productive tasks, you're losing:

- **₹8700 per day** (based on a ₹4350 MVT).
- **₹43500 per week.**
- **Over ₹22,60,000 per year!**

Now ask yourself: What could I do with an extra ₹22,60,000 per year? Would you invest it in better hires, high-impact marketing, or scaling your business? That's the power of prioritizing high-value work.

The Only Similarity Between You and Billionaires: 24 Hours

The world's top billionaires—Elon Musk, Jeff Bezos, Warren Buffett—don't have extra hours in their day. They have the same 24 hours as you. The difference is how they allocate their time:

- **Growth Work:** Strategic decision-making, innovation, networking, scaling, and investing in high-impact opportunities.
- **Operational Work:** Repetitive tasks, admin work, unnecessary meetings, micromanaging employees.

Successful entrepreneurs spend 80% of their time on Growth Work and delegate, automate, or eliminate everything else.

The Choice is Yours: Operational Work or Growth Work?

Every day, you have a choice: Spend your hours on high-value growth activities or get stuck in operational work that someone else could handle.

Start by:

- **Eliminating distractions** (social media, notifications, unnecessary conversations).
- **Delegating low-value tasks** to an EA or team members.
- **Automating repetitive work** using technology.
- **Focusing on strategic, high-return activities** that generate business growth.

Your time is your most expensive resource—guard it fiercely, invest it wisely, and watch your business thrive.

CHAPTER - 6

The Ultimate To-Do List: *Mastering Daily, Weekly, Monthly, and Yearly Planning*

Why To-Do Lists Are Essential for Entrepreneurs

Every successful entrepreneur follows a structured approach to task management. A to-do list is more than just a checklist—it's a productivity system that keeps you on track, ensures nothing important is forgotten, and helps you prioritize high-value activities over trivial tasks.

A well-organized to-do list allows you to:

- **Increase focus** by clearly defining what needs to be done.
- **Improve efficiency** by eliminating decision fatigue.
- **Delegate tasks effectively** to free up time for high-impact work.
- **Stay accountable** and track progress over time.
- **Reduce stress** by removing mental clutter and uncertainty.

A to-do list isn't about doing more—it's about doing what truly matters. Master it, and you master your time.

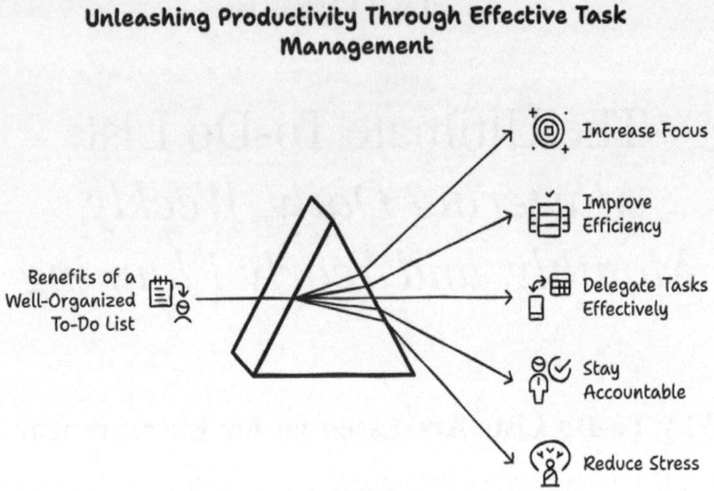

Structuring Your To-Do List: Daily, Weekly, Monthly, and Yearly

To truly optimize your time and maximize productivity, break your to-do list into four key levels:

1. **Daily To-Do List – Tactical Execution**

   Your daily list should focus on specific, actionable tasks that contribute to your larger goals.

   - Prioritize wisely using the **Eisenhower Matrix** (Urgent vs. Important).
   - Assign a time slot for each task (time-blocking method).
   - Limit yourself to **3-5 high-priority tasks** per day to maintain focus.
   - Identify tasks that can be **delegated or automated** to free up your time.

2. **Weekly To-Do List – Strategic Alignment**

   Weekly planning ensures that your daily efforts align with your broader business goals.

   - Review the progress of your **weekly objectives** every Sunday or Monday morning.
   - Schedule deep work sessions for high-impact activities.
   - Plan key meetings and team discussions in advance to avoid last-minute chaos.
   - Identify what worked well the previous week and what needs improvement.
   - **Allocate buffer** time for unexpected challenges or new opportunities.

3. **Monthly To-Do List – High-Level Planning**

   Monthly lists help you evaluate your business growth, track key milestones, and pivot when needed.

   - Review **business performance metrics** (sales, revenue, expenses, etc.).
   - Adjust goals based on new opportunities or challenges.
   - Identify areas for automation or delegation to enhance efficiency.
   - Allocate time for **learning and skill development** to stay ahead.
   - **Celebrate progress!** Acknowledge wins, big or small, to stay motivated.

4. **Yearly To-Do List – Vision and Goal-Setting**

   Your yearly to-do list is about **big-picture thinking** and setting the course for long-term success.

   - Define your clear **annual business goals** (growth, revenue targets, expansion plans).

- Establish personal and professional development goals.
- Identify major investments (hiring, new technology, product launches).
- Plan vacations and breaks to maintain long-term productivity.

Prioritization: The Key to Effective To-Do Lists

Not all tasks hold the same value. One of the biggest mistakes entrepreneurs make is **spending too much time on low-value tasks instead of focusing on high-impact work** that drives real growth. Use these frameworks to prioritize effectively:

- **The 80/20 Rule (Pareto Principle):** 80% of your results come from 20% of your efforts—focus on high-impact tasks.
- **The Eisenhower Matrix:** Categorize tasks as:
  - **Urgent & Important:** Handle immediately.
  - **Important but Not Urgent:** Schedule for later (these drive long-term success).
  - **Urgent but Not Important:** Delegate to free up your time.
  - **Neither Urgent nor Important:** Eliminate to avoid wasting energy.
- **Delegation & Automation:** If a task doesn't require your expertise, delegate or automate it.

The Link Between To-Do Lists and Business Automation

Your to-do list should not just be about **what you need to do**, but also **what you can delegate or automate**.

- **Operational tasks** (follow-ups, scheduling, admin work) should be automated or assigned to an EA.
- **Growth-focused tasks** (strategic planning, sales, innovation) should be where your time is spent.

By mastering your to-do list and linking it to automation and delegation, you'll **optimize your time, increase productivity, and accelerate business growth.** Every minute you reclaim is an opportunity to scale smarter and lead more effectively.

CHAPTER - 7

Cafe Office: *The Growth Day Ritual*

The Concept of Cafe Office

One of the most powerful yet unconventional productivity techniques is the concept of the **Cafe Office**—dedicating **one full day per week** to working from a coffee shop. This practice, taught to me by my coach, has transformed the way I think, strategize, and innovate in my business.

At first, it may sound casual, funny, or even counterintuitive, but this **one small shift** in your weekly routine can lead to **breakthrough results.**

Why Work from a Cafe Once a Week?

Stepping away from your usual office environment and immersing yourself in a **new setting** can unlock deep creativity and allow you to think beyond day-to-day operations. This day should be **100% dedicated to yourself and your business growth.** It's not a day for admin work, emails, or meetings—it's a day to think bigger, strategize, and plan for innovation in your business.

The Science Behind Cafe Office

Research suggests that a **mild level of ambient noise**—such as the background chatter and hum of a coffee shop—can actually **enhance creativity and problem-solving abilities.** When you're in a different environment, your brain **engages in new ways,** helping you break free from the monotony of daily operational work. It forces you to shift from a reactive mode to a **proactive, visionary mindset.**

How to Make the Most of Your Cafe Office Day

1. **Put Your Phone on Airplane Mode**: Eliminate distractions by temporarily disconnecting from calls, messages, and notifications.
2. **Engage in Deep Work**: Use this day to work on high-level business growth tasks, such as innovation, scaling strategies, and creative problem-solving.
3. **Focus on Your Business, Not Just In It**: Avoid mundane tasks like answering emails or handling small admin issues. Instead, dedicate this time to thinking about long-term strategy.
4. **Brainstorm, Plan, and Innovate**: Use this day for product development, service improvements, or customer experience enhancements.

Take Short Breaks – It's okay to check in with your office once or twice, but don't let it consume your time. The goal is **deep, uninterrupted work.**

The Real Impact of Cafe Office Days

Many successful entrepreneurs, including myself, have seen incredible results by implementing this strategy. The key is **consistency**. Doing this sporadically won't yield the same impact—**commit to it every week**, and you'll start noticing exponential growth in your business and mindset.

CHAPTER - 8

Checklists: *The Gold Standard of Automation*

The Power of Checklists in Business

They say **old is gold**, and when it comes to business automation, **checklists are the ultimate gold standard**. They may seem simple, but checklists are one of the most powerful tools for ensuring efficiency, consistency, and scalability in business operations.

- **Eliminate confusion** by providing clear, step-by-step instructions.
- **Reduce errors** and improve quality control.
- **Enhance productivity** by keeping teams aligned and focused.

Whether you're managing daily tasks, onboarding new employees, or executing high-stakes projects, a well-crafted checklist keeps everything on track and optimized for success.

Why Checklists Work

1. **Instant Deployment:** You can create and implement a checklist in minutes—whether on paper or a digital tool.
2. **Scalability:** A well-documented checklist allows your business processes to be replicated effortlessly.

3. **Accountability:** Checklists ensure that nothing is forgotten, reducing the chances of mistakes.
4. **Ease of Use:** Anyone in your team, from entry-level employees to executives, can follow a checklist to complete tasks efficiently.
5. **Automation without Tech:** Checklists are the **simplest form of automation**, ensuring repeatability without requiring expensive software.

Digital vs. Paper Checklists

- **Traditional Paper Checklists** – Classic and effective, they work for those who prefer a hands-on approach.
- **Digital Checklists** – Tools like Trello, Asana, Notion, and Google Keep provide interactive checklists that integrate with your workflow.
- **Hybrid Approach** – Some entrepreneurs use digital checklists for long-term planning and paper checklists for daily execution.

Examples of Business Checklists

- **Daily Operations Checklist** – Ensures smooth execution of recurring tasks.
- **Employee Onboarding Checklist** – Helps new hires integrate seamlessly into company culture and workflow.
- **Sales Process Checklist** – Guides your sales team through prospecting, follow-ups, and closing deals.
- **Client Onboarding Checklist** – Ensures a smooth customer experience from the start.

➢ **Product Launch Checklist** – Covers all aspects from development to marketing and sales.

How to Create Effective Checklists

1. Identify the process that needs standardization.
2. Break it down into clear, actionable steps.
3. Prioritize tasks based on urgency and importance.
4. Test the checklist with your team to ensure usability.
5. Refine and improve it over time based on feedback.
6. Automate where possible (e.g., using digital tools).

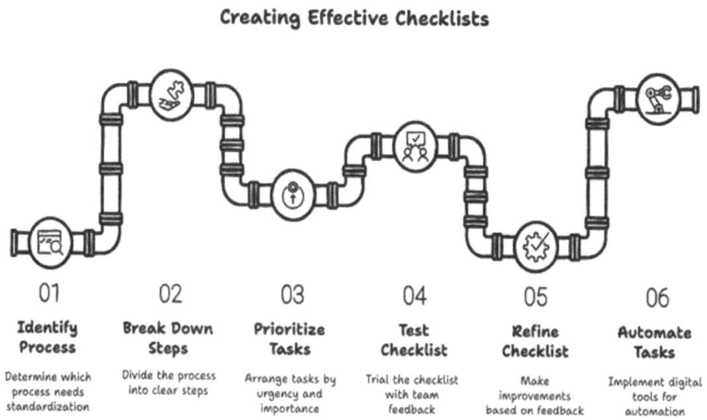

Final Thoughts

A well-designed checklist is a **powerful automation tool** that ensures efficiency, consistency, and productivity in your business. If you're not already using checklists, start today—your business success depends on it.

CHAPTER - 9

SOPs: *Your Foundation of Automation*

The Importance of Standard Operating Procedures (SOPs)

In any successful business, **consistency and efficiency** are key. Standard Operating Procedures (SOPs) provide a **structured framework** that ensures tasks are completed efficiently, correctly, and consistently—regardless of who is performing them.

SOPs are the **foundation of automation**, as they create a clear, step-by-step process for recurring tasks, allowing businesses to scale without chaos.

Why SOPs Are Essential

1. **Scalability:** SOPs allow your business to grow without bottlenecks.
2. **Efficiency:** Tasks are completed faster and with fewer errors.
3. **Training Made Easy:** New employees can quickly adapt by following SOPs.
4. **Seamless Delegation & Automation:** Once documented, tasks can be outsourced or automated.

5. **Quality Control:** Ensures the same high standard of execution across teams.

How to Create Effective SOPs

1. **Identify Key Processes** – Focus on the most repetitive and time-consuming tasks.
2. **Break Down Steps Clearly** – Make each step simple, specific, and actionable.
3. **Use Checklists and Flowcharts** – Visual aids make SOPs easy to follow.
4. **Choose the Right Format** – SOPs can be written documents, video tutorials, or interactive templates, depending on the task.
5. **Test and Optimize** – Ensure the SOP is practical, easy to follow, and adaptable. Update it regularly to keep up with evolving business needs.

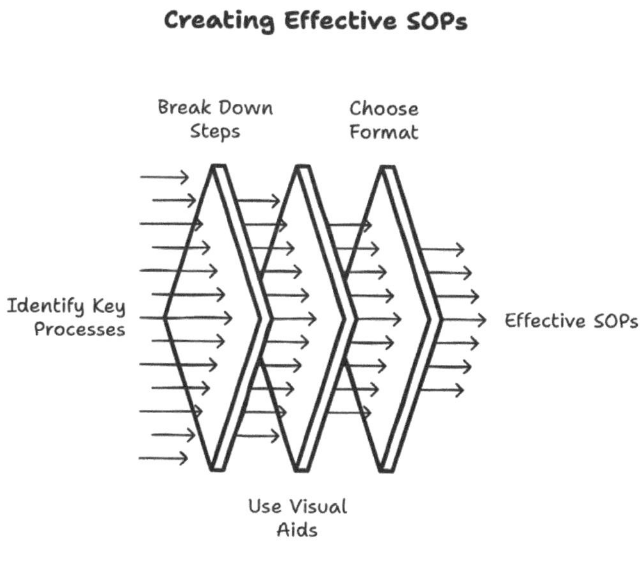

Examples of SOPs in Business

Here are some essential SOPs every business should have:

- **Client Onboarding SOP**: A step-by-step process for welcoming, educating, and integrating new clients to ensure a seamless experience.
- **Social Media SOP**: A detailed guide for content scheduling, posting strategies, engagement, and analytics tracking across platforms.
- **Hiring SOP**: A structured recruitment process to attract, assess, and hire the best talent efficiently.
- **Customer Support SOP**: Predefined responses and troubleshooting steps for handling complaints, inquiries, and customer issues professionally.
- **Sales SOP**: A step-by-step guide for prospecting, nurturing leads, closing deals, and follow-ups, ensuring a consistent sales process.

Final Thoughts

SOPs are the backbone of business automation. They streamline operations, eliminate inefficiencies, and allow your company to scale effortlessly. When implemented correctly, they help businesses run smoothly, allowing teams to focus on growth and innovation instead of daily firefighting.

CHAPTER - 10

The Process Coordinator: *The Backbone of Execution*

The Importance of Standard Operating Procedures (SOPs)

As you move towards automating your business, the first crucial hire is your Executive Assistant (EA)—your right hand who manages almost everything. But once your EA is in place, the next key hire in your journey to automation is your Process Coordinator (PC). She is the second pillar of your second line of leadership, responsible for making sure your Checklists (CLs) and Standard Operating Procedures (SOPs) are being executed seamlessly.

If automation is the foundation of your business's efficiency, then the Process Coordinator is the custodian of that foundation. She doesn't just ensure that things are running smoothly—she enforces your systems with discipline, ensuring that your business operates like a well-oiled machine.

Why a Process Coordinator is Essential

Many entrepreneurs make the mistake of believing that once SOPs and checklists are created, everything will magically run on autopilot. But the truth is, processes are only as strong as the people enforcing them. This is where a Process Coordinator (PC) comes in. She is responsible for ensuring that every system, every checklist, and every procedure is being followed to the letter, every single day.

Without a PC, SOPs are just documents. With a PC, SOPs become the DNA of your business operations.

Think of a Process Coordinator as the operations enforcer—someone who ensures that everything you have put in place continues to function efficiently without you having to micromanage.

A well-trained PC will:

- Ensure SOPs are executed flawlessly
- Oversee daily operations without requiring your direct involvement
- Identify and troubleshoot inefficiencies in the process
- Hold employees accountable for following systems and checklists
- Report critical deviations or breakdowns in processes before they become major issues

Role of a Process Coordinator in Operations

Ensure SOPs are executed flawlessly

The PC guarantees that standard operating procedures are followed perfectly.

Oversee daily operations without requiring your direct involvement

The PC manages daily tasks independently, reducing the need for direct oversight.

Identify and troubleshoot inefficiencies in the process

The PC analyzes and resolves process inefficiencies.

Hold employees accountable for following systems and checklists

The PC ensures that employees adhere to systems and checklists.

Report critical deviations or breakdowns in processes before they become major issues

The PC alerts you to significant process issues early.

Imagine a world where you never have to check whether tasks are being completed, whether team members are following procedures, or whether minor inefficiencies are snowballing into larger problems. That's the reality when you hire a Process Coordinator.

The Key Difference Between a Process Coordinator and an Executive Assistant

A common mistake entrepreneurs make is confusing the role of a Process Coordinator with that of an Executive Assistant. While both are key hires in automation, they serve very distinct functions.

Your EA is your right hand, handling almost everything in the business, acting as your eyes, ears, and voice. She is the one who keeps you organized, manages high-level tasks, and ensures that your focus remains on growth and strategy rather than operational headaches.

Your PC, on the other hand, is a specialist in execution. She is responsible for making sure that SOPs, systems, and checklists aren't just created—but are followed every single day. If your EA is your strategic partner, your PC is your operational backbone.

- The EA ensures that you're focusing on high-value, strategic work.
- The PC ensures that everything in your company is being done exactly the way it should be.
- Think of it this way: Your EA frees up your time, and your PC makes sure your company runs without your direct involvement.

The PC's Role in Business Automation

Hiring a PC isn't just about delegation—it's about ensuring that your company is running like an automated system, where human execution is flawless, consistent, and accountable.

A Process Coordinator takes responsibility for all checklists and SOPs, ensuring that:

- Employees follow SOPs without deviation.
- Mistakes, inefficiencies, and inconsistencies are spotted before they become costly errors.
- All operational processes continue functioning as planned, even if you're away.
- Accountability is built into the system, ensuring that no one can ignore company processes without consequence.
- Employees are trained to work within the system, rather than relying on gut instinct or ad-hoc decision-making.

A great Process Coordinator acts as your company's operating system—ensuring that everything runs smoothly, every day, without fail.

The Cost-Benefit of Hiring a Process Coordinator

Entrepreneurs often hesitate when hiring their PC, thinking it's an unnecessary cost. The truth is, the salary of a PC is a fraction of what you'll save in operational efficiency. Without a PC, you'll constantly be dragged back into daily firefighting, correcting mistakes, and ensuring people are following systems. With a PC, your company will operate independently of you, allowing you to focus on scaling and innovating.

A PC is not an expense—it's an investment in the automation, efficiency, and long-term scalability of your business.

Final Thoughts

The secret to building an automated business isn't just about implementing SOPs or checklists—it's about hiring the right people to enforce them. Your Process Coordinator is the key to ensuring that automation isn't just a concept, but a daily reality in your business.

If you're serious about scaling your company without being trapped in operations, hiring a Process Coordinator is not optional—it's mandatory.

With a great EA and a dedicated PC, your business will run efficiently, systematically, and—most importantly—without you having to micromanage. And that is the real key to true automation and domination in business.

CHAPTER - 11

Budgeting:
The Backbone of Financial Control

In the world of business, especially for small and medium enterprises (SMEs), the saying "What gets measured, gets managed" is more than just a cliché—it is a fundamental principle of financial success. While many business owners focus on revenue growth, very few pay attention to systematic budgeting, which is the key to sustainable profitability and long-term success.

Why Budgeting is Critical for SMEs

For large corporations, budgeting is an ingrained financial discipline, but for SMEs, it is often overlooked due to a lack of structured financial management or a misconception that it limits growth. However, in reality, a well-planned budget serves as a financial blueprint that guides a company's spending, investments, and cost-control efforts.

Without a budget, businesses are often flying blind—spending on impulse rather than strategy. This leads to financial inefficiencies, unnecessary expenses, and cash flow issues that can cripple growth. A budget isn't just about restricting spending—it's about directing resources efficiently to ensure both business sustainability and expansion.

The Science Behind Budgeting: What is Measured, Gets Done

One of the most powerful concepts in business management is that measuring something makes it more likely to be achieved. Just like tracking fitness goals makes it easier to lose weight, tracking financial numbers makes it easier to stay profitable.

A budget provides clarity and control over your business finances, ensuring that every rupee or dollar spent aligns with your company's financial goals. The simple act of measuring and reviewing your expenses regularly will lead to improved decision-making, smarter investments, and a stronger bottom line.

Creating Your Business Budget: Step-by-Step Process

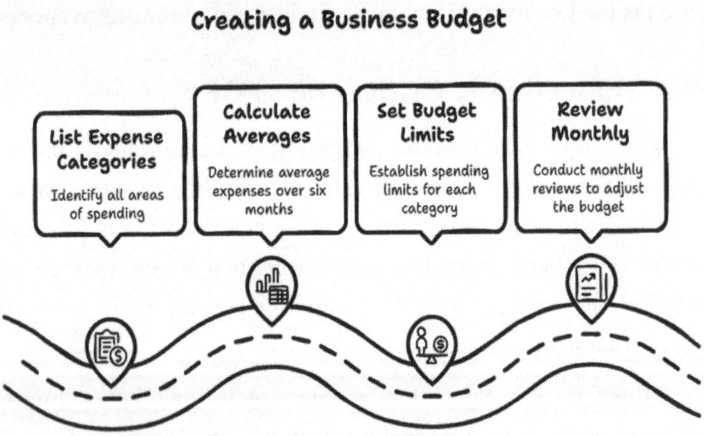

Step 1: List Down All Your Expense Categories (Heads of Expenses)

The first step in budgeting is categorizing your expenses. This means identifying and listing every head of expenditure your business incurs. Proper categorization helps in tracking, controlling, and optimizing costs to improve profitability and cash flow management.

Here are some common business expenses include:

- **Fixed Expenses:** Rent, utilities, salaries, insurance, software subscriptions, loan repayments.
- **Variable Expenses:** Marketing, raw materials, sales commissions, packaging, logistics.
- **Operational Expenses:** Office supplies, repairs, maintenance, training programs.
- **Growth & Expansion Costs:** Research & development, new hires, technology upgrades.
- **Emergency & Contingency Fund:** A financial cushion for unexpected financial hits.

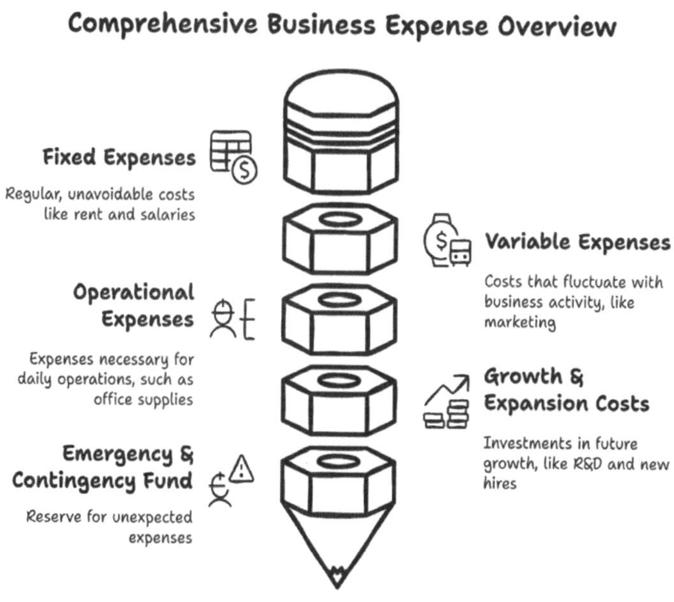

Once all expense heads are listed, you have a clearer picture of where your money is going.

Step 2: Calculate the Average of the Last 6 Months

Now that you have all your expenses categorized, **calculate a 6-month average** for each category. This is your benchmark budget for the coming months. Why six months? Because business expenses fluctuate due to seasonal trends, unexpected costs, and market conditions. A six-month average provides a realistic and balanced view of your actual financial needs.

For example, if your marketing spend fluctuates between ₹50,000 and ₹80,000 per month, your average might be around ₹65,000. This becomes your baseline budget for marketing expenses moving forward.

Step 3: Set Budget Limits for Each Category

Once you have your benchmark, the next step is to set realistic spending limits. If you're overspending in a particular category, consider cutting unnecessary costs or reallocating funds to more productive areas.

For instance, if you're spending too much on office supplies but not enough on marketing, you might reduce the office supply budget and increase marketing investment to drive more business growth.

Step 4: Review Your Budget Monthly

A budget is not a one-time exercise—it must be reviewed and adjusted every month. Compare your actual expenses against your budgeted numbers, analyze any deviations, and take corrective action if needed.

Regular budget reviews will help you:

- Identify unnecessary expenses and eliminate them.
- Improve cash flow management.
- Allocate funds to the highest ROI activities.
- Ensure financial stability and avoid business crises.

The Impact of Budgeting on Business Success

When an SME operates without a structured budget, financial chaos is inevitable. Business owners often find themselves short on cash, struggling to pay salaries, or unable to invest in growth opportunities. However, with proper budgeting in place, businesses experience the following benefits:

1. **Better Financial Control**: You know where your money is going, ensuring that no resources are wasted.
2. **Smarter Decision-Making**: Budgeting helps prioritize investments and cut unnecessary expenses.
3. **Higher Profit Margins**: Tracking expenses helps in optimizing costs and improving profitability.
4. **Reduced Stress & Uncertainty**: Financial predictability leads to peace of mind and smoother business operations.
5. **Stronger Business Growth**: Proper fund allocation ensures that growth initiatives are well-funded and executed.

Final Thoughts

Budgeting is not just for large enterprises—it is an absolute necessity for SMEs aiming for long-term success. Without a structured budget, businesses struggle with cash flow issues, overspending, and financial inefficiencies.

If you want to scale your business without financial headaches, start tracking, setting benchmarks, and reviewing your budget regularly. It's a simple but powerful tool that will help you control expenses, improve profitability, and make informed financial decisions.

In business, money is your fuel—don't waste it, manage it. A well-structured budget is your roadmap to financial success!

CHAPTER - 12

Cost Cutting:
Turning Efficiency into Habit

Cost-cutting isn't just about slashing expenses—it's about creating a culture of financial efficiency and sustainability. For SMEs, where profit margins are often tight, optimizing costs can mean the difference between thriving and barely surviving.

A well-structured cost-cutting program ensures that resources are being used efficiently while maintaining operational effectiveness. The key is to reduce waste without compromising quality or growth.

Why Cost Cutting is Essential for SMEs

Many SMEs operate under the misconception that revenue growth alone determines profitability. However, businesses that fail to manage and reduce unnecessary expenses often find themselves struggling, even with rising revenue.

Implementing a structured cost-cutting strategy provides numerous benefits:

1. **Increased Profitability**: Every rupee saved goes directly to the bottom line.
2. **Improved Cash Flow**: More available cash means better financial flexibility.

3. **Operational Efficiency**: Eliminating waste ensures smoother business operations.
4. **Higher Competitiveness**: A leaner business model allows for better pricing and investment in innovation.
5. **Stronger Resilience**: Businesses with controlled costs can withstand economic downturns better.

The Science of Cost Cutting: Structured & Sustainable

The six-month benchmark you set during the budgeting process serves as the foundation for cost-cutting. Here's how you turn it into an effective, measurable program:

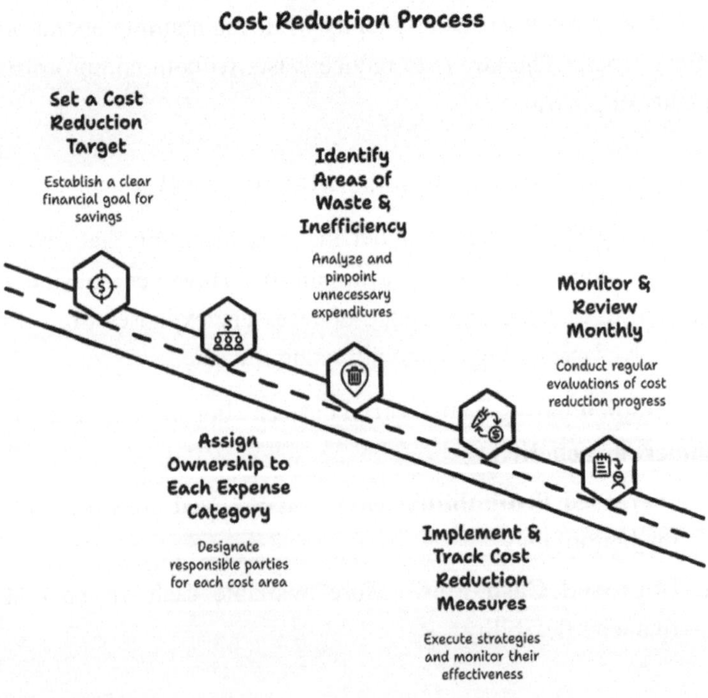

Step 1: Set a Cost Reduction Target

- Review your six-month expense benchmark and determine a realistic percentage reduction.
- Common reduction targets range between 5% to 15%, depending on business size, industry, and current efficiency levels.
- Ensure targets are achievable without sacrificing quality, efficiency, or customer satisfaction.

Step 2: Assign Ownership to Each Expense Category

- Every cost category (rent, utilities, marketing, raw materials, logistics, etc.) should have a dedicated owner.
- Assign one responsible person per cost head who will oversee and drive reduction efforts, you can even merge 3-4 of them if you have limited people.
- Ownership creates accountability, ensuring that cost-cutting becomes an active, ongoing responsibility, not just a one-time effort.

Step 3: Identify Areas of Waste & Inefficiency

- Audit past expenses and identify unnecessary spending.
- Common cost-cutting areas include:
    - **Office Supplies & Subscriptions**: Cut down on unused tools and services.
    - **Marketing Spend**: Optimize ad campaigns, shift towards high-ROI channels, and eliminate ineffective channels.
    - **Utility & Energy Costs**: Switch to energy-efficient solutions.
    - **Procurement & Vendor Contracts**: Negotiate better deals, seek bulk discounts, and explore alternative suppliers.

- **Operational Processes**: Automate repetitive tasks, reduce manual work, and streamline workflows.

Step 4: Implement & Track Cost Reduction Measures

- Develop an action plan for each cost head, listing specific reduction steps.
- Introduce monthly reviews where cost owners report progress and impact.
- Utilize software or spreadsheets to track and compare actual vs. targeted reductions.

Step 5: Monitor & Review Monthly

- Review each expense category every month to ensure cost-cutting measures are being implemented.
- Celebrate small wins and encourage a cost-conscious mindset among employees.
- Refine strategies based on results and adjust targets as needed.

The Impact of Continuous Cost Cutting

A structured cost-cutting approach doesn't just reduce expenses—it builds financial discipline into your company's DNA. The long-term impact includes:

- **Sustainable Growth**: Lower costs free up capital for strategic investments.
- **Competitive Edge**: Businesses that control costs can offer better pricing and stay ahead.
- **Stronger Profit Margins**: Leaner operations lead to healthier financial performance.
- **More Resources for Innovation**: Money saved can be redirected to R&D, new product development, process automation, or customer experience improvements.

Final Thoughts

Cost-cutting is not a one-time exercise; it is a habit that should be ingrained into your business culture. When done right, it enhances efficiency, strengthens financial health, and ultimately makes your business more resilient and profitable.

Start today—set your targets, assign cost owners, and make monthly cost reviews a non-negotiable business practice. Remember, the most successful businesses are not just the ones that generate the most revenue, but the ones that manage and optimize their expenses effectively. Financial efficiency is the key to sustained success!

CHAPTER - 13

Profit Myths: *Understanding Profits for Business Success*

Many business owners in India focus solely on increasing sales, believing that higher sales automatically lead to higher profits. However, this is a common misconception. Profitability is not just about revenue—it's about how efficiently you manage costs, control expenses and retain earnings.

Understanding profitability metrics is crucial for making informed financial decisions, ensuring long-term growth, and maintaining a financially healthy business. Let's break down the key concepts of profit in a clear, simple, and actionable way.

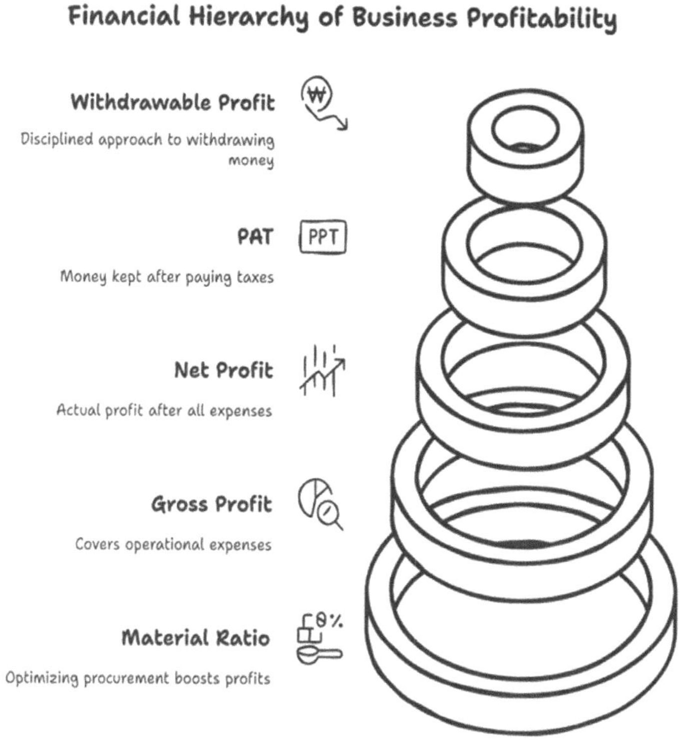

1. Material to Sales Ratio: The First Profitability Indicator

One of the most critical metrics in product-based businesses is the Material to Sales Ratio. This ratio helps you understand how much of your sales revenue is consumed by raw material costs.

Why is it Important?

- **Cost Control:** A high ratio indicates excessive spending on raw materials, highlighting the need for better supplier negotiations or cost-cutting strategies.
- **Pricing Strategy:** Understanding this ratio helps in setting competitive and profitable prices.

- **Profit Margin Optimization:** Keeping material costs in check leads to improved overall profitability.

Formula:

$$MaterialtoSalesRatio = \left(\frac{TotalMaterialCost}{TotalSales}\right) \times 100$$

Example: If your total sales for a month are **₹10,00,000**, and your raw material cost is **₹4,00,000**, then:

$$MaterialtoSalesRatio = \left(\frac{4,00,000}{10,00,000}\right) \times 100 = 40\%$$

A lower percentage means better efficiency, while a higher ratio suggests the need for cost reduction or supplier renegotiation.

2. **Gross Profit – The First Level of Profitability**

Gross Profit is what remains after deducting the direct costs of production (raw materials, labor, and direct expenses) from total sales.

Formula:

$$GrossProfit = TotalSales - CostofGoodsSold(COGS)$$

Example: If your total sales are **₹10,00,000**, and your direct costs (COGS) are **₹6,00,000**, then:

$$GrossProfit = 10,00,000 - 6,00,000 = ₹4,00,000$$

A strong gross profit margin is essential because it determines your ability to cover operational expenses and generate net profits.

Gross Profit Margin Formula:

$$GrossProfitMargin = \left(\frac{GrossProfit}{TotalSales}\right) \times 100$$

In this case:

$$GrossProfitMargin = \left(\frac{4,00,000}{10,00,000}\right) \times 100 = 40\%$$

Why Gross Profit Matters:

- **Indicates pricing effectiveness:** A healthy margin ensures you are pricing your products correctly.
- **Supports operational expenses:** Covers rent, marketing, and salaries.
- **Drives business growth:** Higher margins allow for expansion and innovation.

3. **Net Profit – The Real Business Profit**

While gross profit is important, **Net Profit is what truly matters** because it accounts for all expenses, including rent, salaries, marketing, utilities, and overhead costs. It reflects the actual earnings a business retains after all deductions.

Formula:

$$NetProfit = GrossProfit - OperatingExpenses$$
$$- Taxes - Interest$$

Example: If your **gross profit** is **₹4,00,000**, and your operating expenses (rent, salaries, marketing, etc.) are **₹2,50,000**, and taxes & interest amount to **₹50,000**, then:

$$NetProfit = 4,00,000 - (2,50,000 + 50,000) = ₹1,00,000$$

Net Profit Margin Formula:

$$NetProfitMargin = \left(\frac{NetProfit}{TotalSales}\right) \times 100$$

In this case:

$$NetProfitMargin = \left(\frac{1,00,000}{10,00,000}\right) \times 100 = 10\%$$

Why Net Profit Matters:

- **Shows true business profitability**: Determines whether a company is financially strong.
- **Affects business valuation**: Investors and lenders evaluate net profit for funding decisions.
- **Supports future growth**: A strong net profit allows for expansion, hiring, and reinvestment.

A business must maintain a healthy net profit margin to remain sustainable and scalable.

4. **PAT (Profit After Tax) – The Final Profit Figure**

Profit After Tax (PAT) is the final amount left after paying all business-related taxes. It represents the actual earnings that can be reinvested in the business or distributed to stakeholders.

Formula:

$$PAT = NetProfit - Taxes$$

Example: If your Net Profit is ₹1,00,000 and your Tax is ₹20,000, then:

$$PAT = 1,00,000 - 20,000 = ₹80,000$$

Why PAT Matters:

- **Reflects true profitability**: PAT shows the final earnings after all deductions.

- **Essential for reinvestment**: A higher PAT allows for business expansion and innovation.
- **Determines shareholder returns**: Investors and stakeholders focus on PAT for financial decisions.

A strong PAT margin ensures that the business remains financially stable and growth-ready in the long run!

5. **Withdrawable Profit – How Much Can You Take Home?**

One of the biggest mistakes business owners make is withdrawing too much profit from the business, leading to cash flow issues. Maintaining a balance between personal income and business needs is crucial for long-term sustainability.

A simple **rule of thumb** for sustainable withdrawals:

- **50% of Net Profit** should be reinvested for growth.
- **30% of Net Profit** can be taken as personal income.
- **20% of Net Profit** should be kept as a buffer for emergencies.

Example: If your PAT is ₹80,000, then:

- **₹40,000** should be reinvested.
- **₹24,000** can be withdrawn.
- **₹16,000** should remain as a buffer.

This strategy ensures that your business remains financially healthy while you also enjoy the rewards of your hard work.

Key Takeaways: Mastering Profits in Business

1. **Material to Sales Ratio**: Keep an eye on raw material costs; optimizing procurement can boost profits.
2. **Gross Profit**: The first profitability level; helps you cover operational expenses.

3. **Net Profit**: The actual business profit after all expenses.
4. **PAT (Profit After Tax)**: The real money you keep after paying taxes.
5. **Withdrawable Profit**: Maintain a disciplined approach to taking money from your business.

Understanding these profit metrics ensures that you don't just run a business—you run a profitable one. Always track, measure, and optimize your profitability for long-term success.

CHAPTER - 14

Game-Changing Marketing: *How to Make Your Business Irresistible*

If you want your business to grow exponentially, you must stop marketing like everyone else. Traditional advertising is losing its impact, and customers today don't want to be sold to—they want to connect, engage, and believe in something bigger.

This chapter will break down how to create marketing that makes people say "Wow, I NEED this!" instead of ignoring your brand. If you apply these principles, your business will become so unique and compelling that customers will market it for you.

Innovative Marketing Strategies

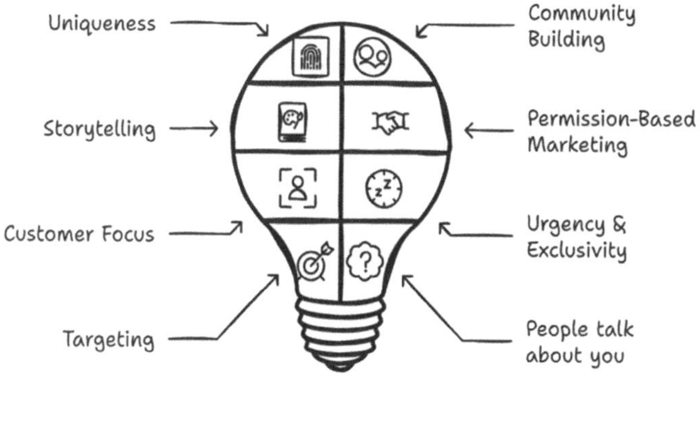

Stand Out by Being Unique, Not Just Better

Imagine walking into a marketplace where every shop looks the same, sells the same products, and shouts the same discounts. You ignore them. But suddenly, you see a store that looks different, speaks differently, and offers something you haven't seen before. That's the store you remember.

Marketing is no longer about just being "better" than competitors—it's about being different and unforgettable.

ACTION STEP: Ask yourself, *What makes my business so unique that people can't help but talk about it?*

Example: A bakery that sells only monochrome cakes. A car dealership that offers a free road trip package with every car. A financial planner who does consultations in a luxury lounge setting instead of a dull office. Make your business the one people remember.

Build a Community, Not Just Customers

Marketing isn't about pushing products—it's about pulling people into an experience. Customers today want to feel like they belong to something meaningful.

Idea: The strongest brands don't just sell products; they build a community of loyal supporters who feel connected.

ACTION STEP: Turn your customers into a movement.

Example: A yoga studio that offers free sunrise sessions for members every weekend. A clothing brand that hosts exclusive styling events for top customers. A coaching business that builds a private WhatsApp community for ongoing support and networking.

Sell Stories, Not Just Products

People don't buy things—they buy feelings, experiences, and transformations. Your brand story is what makes your product resonate with customers.

ACTION STEP: Answer these questions to create your brand story:

- Why did you start this business?
- What problem are you solving?
- How does your product make life better for your customers?
- What values drive your business?

Example: A skincare brand that started because the founder couldn't find clean, chemical-free products for her child. A restaurant that sources 100% organic, local ingredients from small farmers. Your story is your marketing superpower. Use it to make your brand **irresistible**.

Permission-Based Marketing: Let Customers Come to You

Traditional advertising interrupts people. Modern marketing invites them in. Instead of chasing customers, build a system where they want to hear from you.

ACTION STEP: Build a permission-based marketing system:

- Start an email list or WhatsApp broadcast group.
- Offer something valuable in exchange for contact details (free guides, knowledge, transformative content, early access, VIP perks etc).

➢ Provide consistent, high-value content so customers stay engaged.

Example: A real estate consultant who shares weekly market insights via WhatsApp, keeping clients engaged until they're ready to buy. Be valuable before asking for a sale.

NEXT-LEVEL STRATEGY

Micro-Commitments: Get customers to say small yeses before a big purchase.

Example: A car dealer offering a 30-second quiz to match customers with their ideal car.

Make Your Customers Feel Like the Main Character

Your marketing shouldn't be about how great you are—it should be about how your customers win with your product.

ACTION STEP: Shift your marketing from *"Look at us"* to *"Look at what you can achieve with us"*

Example: Instead of a gym posting "We have the best trainers," post "Meet Rahul—he lost 20 kgs and transformed his life in 3 months with our program!" Make your customers the hero of your story.

Create Urgency & Exclusivity

People act faster when they fear missing out. If your product feels **limited, exclusive, or time-sensitive**, customers will be more likely to buy.

ACTION STEP: Introduce limited-time offers, VIP access, or exclusive product drops.

Example: A fashion brand that releases new collections only for VIP members before public sales. A consulting business that takes only 10 clients per quarter. Make people feel lucky to be your customer.

Target the Right Customers, Not Everyone

Trying to market to everyone is a mistake. The secret? Find your perfect audience and speak directly to them.

ACTION STEP: Define your smallest viable audience. Ask yourself:

- Who are my biggest fans?
  - Typically, they will be high profit giving and would repeatedly give reference.
- What do they want more of?
  - Make a list of such customers and talk to them, ask their challenges and see how you can solve their problem or be useful to them.
- How can I serve them better than anyone else?
  - The answer lies in talking to your biggest fans.

Example: A cafe that markets only to students by offering "Late Night Study Specials." A personal trainer who focuses only on busy corporate professionals. Narrow your focus, dominate your niche.

Marketing is About What People Say When You're Not in the Room

Your brand isn't what you say about it—it's what your customers say about it when you're not there. Make sure they have something worth talking about.

Final Action Steps:

- **Be Remarkable:** Stand out in a way that makes people remember you.
- **Build a Tribe:** Customers come and go—communities stay.
- **Sell Stories, Not Just Products:** Facts tell, but stories sell.
- **Earn Attention, Don't Demand It:** Get permission before selling.
- **Make Your Customers the Heroes:** Their success is your best marketing.
- **Create Urgency & Exclusivity:** People want what feels rare.
- **Target the Right People:** Speak to those who truly need your product.

Marketing today isn't about spending more on ads—it's about creating something so compelling that people can't ignore it. If you apply these principles, your business won't just sell products—it will create a lasting movement.

CHAPTER - 15

Revenue Growth Strategies: *Making More Without Working More*

Many small and medium business owners believe that increasing revenue means working harder, putting in more hours, or expanding operations. But in reality, revenue growth doesn't have to mean more effort—it just requires smarter strategies.

The most successful businesses don't just focus on getting more customers; they focus on making more from the customers they already have while ensuring that their pricing is structured for maximum profitability.

Sell High-Value Offers Instead of Low-Margin Products/Services

One of the biggest mistakes SMEs make is competing on price. Many business owners believe that lowering prices will attract more customers, but this often leads to lower profits and more stress. Instead of lowering prices, focus on creating high-value offers that justify a premium price.

How to Create a High-Value Offer

A high-value offer is one that:

- Solves a bigger problem for the customer.
- Has additional benefits or premium elements that justify a higher price.
- Increases customer trust and confidence in your product/service.

Example: A printing shop used to compete on price, selling 500 business cards for ₹500. They shifted their approach by offering "Premium Business Card Packages" that included:

- Custom-designed business cards with high-end materials.
- QR code linking to their website or portfolio.
- A personal consultation for branding advice.

Instead of selling 500 cards for ₹500, they started selling their premium package for ₹2,500 (5X increase!), with minimal additional effort. The result? Higher revenue per customer and better margins.

Action Step

- Identify one product/service in your business where you can add value instead of lowering price.

- Package it differently, add a small premium element, and test a higher price.
- Observe how customers react—you'll be surprised how many are willing to pay more for perceived value.

Pricing Strategy – Charge What You're Worth

Many SMEs set prices based on competition instead of value. The problem with this approach? It leads to a race to the bottom, where businesses undercut each other and end up with low margins and high stress.

The Right Way to Price Your Products/Services

Instead of focusing on being the cheapest, focus on being the best value in your industry.

- **Cost-Plus Pricing**: Add a fair profit margin on top of your costs.
- **Value-Based Pricing**: Price based on the customer's perceived value, not just your costs.
- **Tiered Pricing**: Offer different pricing levels (Basic, Premium, VIP) to capture different types of customers.

Example: A coaching business was charging ₹5,000 for a basic training course. They introduced a three-tier pricing model:

- **Basic Course – ₹5,000** (Self-paced video lessons)
- **Premium Course – ₹10,000** (Includes live Q&A sessions)
- **VIP Course – ₹20,000** (Includes 1-on-1 coaching + personalized strategy)

Outcome? Instead of just selling ₹5,000 packages, many customers chose the ₹10,000 and ₹20,000 options, significantly increasing revenue.

Action Step:

- Review your current pricing. Are you underpricing?
- Can you create pricing tiers to offer more value and make more per customer?
- Test different price points and see what works best for your audience.

Upselling & Cross-Selling – Get More From Each Customer

Did you know that it's 5-10 times cheaper to sell to an existing customer than to acquire a new one? The easiest way to increase revenue without extra effort is by selling more to the customers you already have.

Upselling vs. Cross-Selling

- **Upselling** = Selling a higher-priced version of what the customer is already buying.
- **Cross-Selling** = Selling additional products/services that complement what they're buying.

Example: A bakery selling cakes started offering "Cake Upgrade Packages."

- **Regular Cake** – ₹800
- **Upsell:** Premium Cake with Decorations – ₹1,200
- **Cross-Sell:** Add a Gift Box & Greeting Card – ₹300 extra.

Instead of just selling a ₹800 cake, they now make ₹1,500 per customer with small additional offers.

Action Step:

- Identify 1-2 ways you can upsell or cross-sell to your customers.
- Train your team to suggest upgrades or add-ons naturally, not forcefully.

Increase Repeat Business – Your Existing Customers Are Gold

Many businesses focus too much on getting new customers but ignore keeping their existing ones. Loyal customers not only spend more but also refer others, driving consistent business growth.

Ways to Increase Repeat Business

- **Customer Loyalty Programs:** Give small rewards for repeat purchases. Offer points, discounts, or special perks.
- **Follow-Up Emails, Messages, Calls**: Stay in touch with customers after they buy. Remind customers of your services and offer personalized deals.
- **Subscription & Retainer Models**: Get customers on monthly or yearly plans.

Example: A salon introduced a Monthly Membership Plan for ₹999, which included:

- 2 free haircuts
- 10% discount on all services
- Priority appointments

Instead of waiting for customers to return, they locked in monthly revenue upfront while keeping clients engaged.

Action Step

- ➢ Identify one way to increase repeat business from your current customers—whether through loyalty programs, follow-ups, or subscriptions.

Final Thoughts – Focus on Smart Growth

The biggest mistake SMEs make is believing that more revenue means more effort. The truth is: A high-value offer makes more money than a cheap product. Pricing strategies can boost revenue without new customers. Upselling & cross-selling can double your revenue from existing buyers. Loyalty programs create steady repeat income.

Instead of working harder, work smarter. Apply one or two of these strategies, test them, and watch your business revenue grow without increasing stress.

CHAPTER - 16

Customer Acquisition & Retention: *Winning High-Paying Customers and Keeping Them for Life*

For many small and medium-sized business owners, getting more customers is a top priority. However, the real secret to long-term business success isn't just about attracting new customers—it's about keeping them, increasing their lifetime value, and turning them into loyal advocates.

Most businesses make the mistake of focusing only on customer acquisition and completely ignore retention. Acquiring a new customer costs 5-10 times more than keeping an existing one, yet many SMEs fail to invest in customer experience and loyalty.

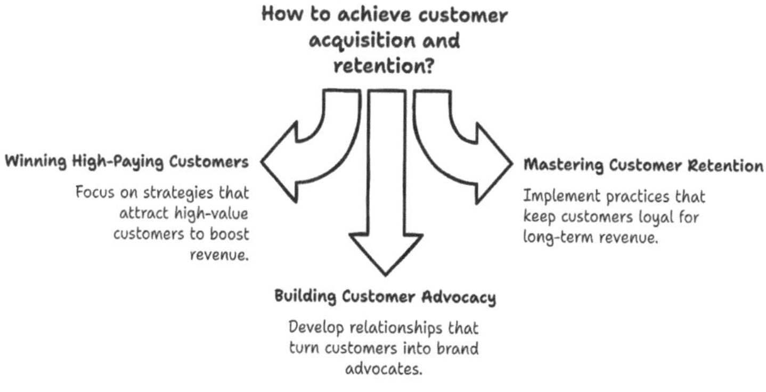

In this chapter, we'll cover proven strategies to attract high-paying customers, keep them for life, and maximize their value to your business.

The Formula for Winning High-Paying Customers

High-paying customers are different from bargain hunters. They value quality over price and are willing to pay a premium for businesses that offer superior service and expertise. To attract them, you need the right positioning, messaging, and strategy.

Step 1: Position Yourself as a Specialist, Not a Generalist

High-paying customers don't look for generalists—they look for experts. Instead of being "just another" service provider, narrow your niche and position yourself as the best in a specific area.

Example: Instead of a generic tractor dealership, specialize in precision-agriculture solutions equipped with smart technology to become the go-to choice for modern, tech-savvy farmers.

Step 2: Use High-Ticket Offerings & Premium Pricing

- Instead of selling low-cost, high-volume services, create a premium package that delivers massive value.
- Offer done-for-you solutions instead of just consulting.
- Use tiered pricing with high-end options to attract premium customers.

Example: A fitness coach shifted from ₹1,500 per session to a ₹50,000 per month transformation package with personal meal plans, 24/7 WhatsApp support, and video check-ins. He now works with fewer customers but makes 10x more.

Step 3: Build a Strong Personal Brand & Authority

People buy from those they trust and respect. Your reputation is your best marketing asset. Build credibility by:

- Creating valuable content (blogs, videos, case studies).
- Speaking at industry events and networking with high-value customers.
- Publishing testimonials and success stories.

People want to work with trusted experts. By showcasing your knowledge and building your authority, you become the go-to choice for premium customers.

Example: A business consultant started posting weekly LinkedIn insights on scaling businesses. Within 6 months, he gained 200+ inquiries from CEOs, purely from content authority.

Mastering Customer Retention – The Key to Long-Term Revenue

Most businesses spend all their efforts on acquiring customers but lose them due to poor experience. The real money isn't in the first transaction—it's in the long-term relationship.

Step 1: Onboard Customers Like a Pro

The first 7 days set the tone for the entire relationship. Customers must feel confident and valued from Day 1.

How to onboard effectively:

- Send a welcome package (email, WhatsApp, guide, or call).
- Clearly define next steps, timelines, and expectations.
- Assign a dedicated point of contact for smooth communication.

Example: A software company reduced customer churn by 40% simply by adding a structured onboarding sequence with a kickoff call, step-by-step guides, and proactive check-ins.

Step 2: Deliver More Than Expected

Surprising your customers with unexpected value can transform them into lifelong loyalists. Don't just meet expectations—exceed them.

How to exceed expectations:

- **Surprise with bonus value**: Think of offering free audits, early access to new features, or exclusive discounts.
- **Provide proactive support**: Instead of waiting for issues to arise, offer assistance before they're needed.
- **Solve problems before they arise**: Stay one step ahead by anticipating customer needs.

Example: A legal consultant started giving quarterly compliance checkups for free. Customers renewed contracts automatically because they felt well taken care of.

Step 3: Build Emotional Loyalty Through Personalization

People stay loyal to businesses that make them feel special. Personal touches go a long way in building emotional connections.

How to personalize for loyalty:

- Send handwritten thank-you notes or small gifts.
- Remember birthdays, milestones, and anniversaries.
- Make personal check-ins part of your system.

Example: A high-end tailor sent a birthday gift to VIP customers with a personalized note. 85% of them came back for repeat orders.

Relationship-Building: How to Turn Customers into Advocates

The ultimate growth hack isn't more marketing—it's turning existing customers into your salesforce. High-paying customers trust referrals more than ads.

Step 1: Build a Referral System

Referrals are one of the most effective ways to attract high-value customers. A referral system incentivizes your existing customers to bring in new business.

- Give incentives for referrals (discounts, exclusive access, or cash bonuses).
- Make it effortless—send a pre-written email/message they can share.
- Publicly appreciate your best referrers.

Example: A premium salon introduced a VIP Referral Club, where each referral earned free services. This led to a 300% increase in referrals within a year.

Step 2: Create a Strong Customer Community

Customers become more loyal when they feel they're part of an exclusive group. A sense of belonging encourages them to stay engaged and refer others.

- Start a private group for top customers (WhatsApp, Facebook, or LinkedIn).
- Host customer-only networking events.
- Give early access to new offers.

Example: A business coach created an inner circle mastermind for top customers. Members stayed longer, spent more, and brought in numerous referrals.

Step 3: Stay in Touch Beyond Business

Building high-value relationships means interacting beyond just business transactions. Show your customers you care about them as people, not just clients.

- Invite customers to dinners, private meetups, or industry events.
- Send them valuable business insights and updates.
- Check in just to ask how they're doing.

Example: A financial planner made it a habit to call 5 customers per week just to chat. Within a year, his customer retention doubled.

Final Thoughts – Keep Customers, Keep Growing

Most businesses focus heavily on getting new customers, but the real money lies in keeping the ones you already have.

- Position yourself as an expert to attract high-paying customers.
- Deliver premium service & pricing to maximize value.
- Onboard like a pro & exceed expectations to keep customers for life.
- Use referrals & relationship-building to turn customers into your salesforce.

High-paying customers are looking for reliability, expertise, and relationships—not just a service. Master these strategies, and you won't just grow your revenue—you'll create a business that thrives on long-term success.

CHAPTER - 17

Delegation & Building a Leadership Team: *From Solopreneur to CEO*

Many small and medium business owners start their journey as solopreneurs, juggling every aspect of their business—from sales and marketing to operations and customer service. While this might work in the early stages, trying to do everything yourself will eventually limit your business growth.

The transition from being a solopreneur to a CEO is one of the most critical steps in scaling your business. It requires learning how to delegate effectively and building a strong leadership team that can run the business without your constant involvement.

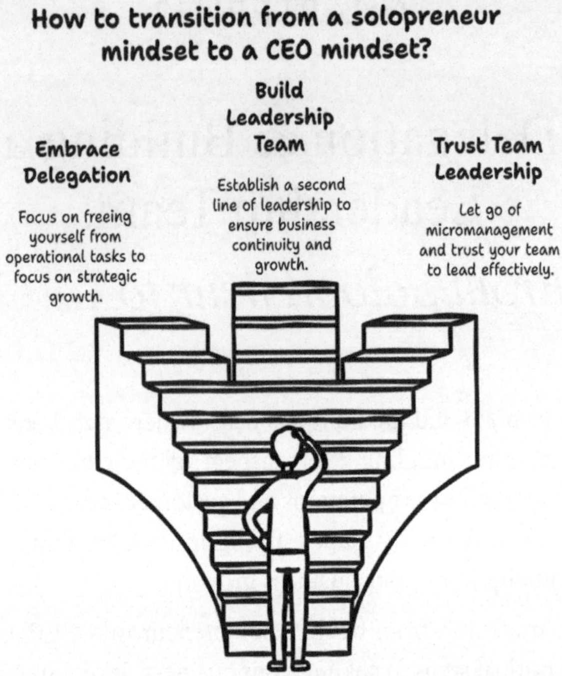

In this chapter, we'll explore how to shift your mindset, delegate tasks strategically, and create a second line of leadership that ensures your business operates smoothly and grows sustainably.

Moving from a Solopreneur Mindset to a CEO Mindset

As a solopreneur, you wear every hat—marketer, salesperson, customer support, and even HR. While this might work for a while, it eventually leads to burnout and limits your business growth. It's time to break free from this cycle and step into the role of CEO, where you lead your business toward sustainable growth without getting caught in every operational detail.

The Solopreneur Trap: Why Doing Everything Yourself Holds You Back

You've built your business from the ground up, and it's hard to trust others with your "baby." But this mindset is what keeps many businesses stuck at a small scale.

Here's why doing everything yourself is a trap:

- **Limited Time = Limited Growth:** You only have 24 hours in a day. The more time you spend on routine tasks, the less time you have for strategic growth.
- **Burnout Risk:** Trying to manage every aspect of your business leads to stress and exhaustion.
- **Bottleneck Effect:** When all decisions flow through you, your business slows down and opportunities slip through the cracks.

The CEO Mindset: Focus on Growth, Not Operations

A CEO's primary role is to lead, strategize, and grow the business—not to manage day-to-day tasks.

Shifting to a CEO mindset means:

1. **Trusting Others:** Realizing that other people can handle tasks—even better than you in some cases. Delegate with confidence.
2. **Focusing on High-Value Activities:** Spending your time on tasks that directly contribute to business growth (e.g., strategic planning, networking, innovation).

3. **Building Systems:** Creating processes and systems that allow the business to run without your constant oversight.
4. **Mindset Shift Example:** Instead of spending 2 hours a day responding to emails, use that time to build partnerships, explore new markets, or innovate your offerings.

The Art of Delegation – Freeing Yourself from Operational Tasks

Delegation isn't just about passing off tasks—it's about assigning the right tasks to the right people, so you can focus on what truly matters.

What to Delegate (and What to Keep)

- **Delegate:**
  - Administrative tasks (emails, scheduling, data entry)
  - Routine operations (inventory management, invoicing, customer support)
  - Marketing execution (social media posts, ad management)
  - Follow-ups and coordination
- **Keep (CEO-Level Tasks):**
  - Strategic planning
  - Business development & partnerships
  - Financial oversight & high-level decision-making
  - Leadership and team development

How to Delegate Effectively

1. **Start Small:** Begin by delegating simple, time-consuming tasks. As you gain confidence in your team, you can delegate more critical responsibilities.

2. **Document Processes:** Create Checklists (CLs) and Standard Operating Procedures (SOPs) to guide your team. This ensures consistency and reduces errors.
3. **Assign Ownership:** Don't just assign tasks—assign responsibility for outcomes. Make sure they understand how their work impacts the larger business goals.
4. **Communicate Clearly:** Be clear about what's expected in terms of quality, deadlines, and deliverables. Effective communication prevents confusion and ensures better results.
5. **Trust but Verify:** Once delegated, trust your team to get the job done, but don't hesitate to check in on their progress. Set up regular check-ins to monitor progress without micromanaging.

Example: Instead of micromanaging your social media, create a clear SOP and assign a team member to handle content posting, while you focus on strategy.

Building a Second Line of Leadership Beyond EA & PC

Once you've hired your Executive Assistant (EA) and Process Coordinator (PC), the next step is to build a second line of leadership—a team that can take over key areas of your business, allowing you to step back from daily operations.

Key Roles in Your Leadership Team

1. **Operations Manager**
    - Oversees daily business activities.
    - Ensures that SOPs and processes are followed.
    - Manages staff and resources for smooth operations.

2. **Sales & Marketing Manager**
   - Develops and executes sales strategies.
   - Manages marketing campaigns and customer acquisition.
   - Tracks performance metrics and adjusts strategies accordingly.
3. **Finance Manager**
   - Handles budgeting, financial planning, and reporting.
   - Manages cash flow, expenses, and cost optimization.
   - Ensures compliance with tax and legal regulations.
4. **Human Resources (HR) Manager**
   - Manages recruitment, onboarding, and employee development.
   - Ensures a healthy workplace culture.
   - Handles conflict resolution and employee satisfaction.
5. **Customer Relationship Manager**
   - Focuses on **retaining clients** and ensuring they are satisfied.
   - Handles complaints, feedback, and customer loyalty programs.
   - Builds strong relationships with key clients.

How to Identify and Develop Leaders from Within

Building leadership from within your organization can save time, resources, and boost morale. You don't always need to hire from outside. Often, the best leaders are already within your organization.

1. **Identify Potential Leaders:** Look for the individuals who exhibit traits that align with effective leadership. While technical skills are important, these personal attributes are often key indicators of leadership potential.

- **Initiative**: Leaders take action without being told, proposing solutions to problems before they escalate.
- **Problem-Solving Skills**: They think critically, offering creative solutions to challenges.
- **Reliability**: They consistently meet expectations and deliver results on time.
- **Alignment with Company Values**: Their behavior and decisions reflect the company's mission, vision, and values, even when no one is watching.

2. **Develop Leadership Skills**: Once you've identified potential leaders, the next step is to nurture their growth. This involves providing opportunities for them to develop the skills needed to excel in a leadership role.
    - **Provide Mentorship and Training**: Pair them with senior leaders who can guide and teach them the nuances of leadership.
    - **Give Ownership of Small Projects**: Entrust them with managing small projects or teams, allowing them to practice decision-making and problem-solving in real-world scenarios.
    - **Encourage Decision-Making**: Allow them to take charge of decisions, while offering constructive feedback to build their confidence and refine their approach.
3. **Promote from Within**: When potential leaders have proven themselves, it's time to promote them to managerial or leadership roles. Internal promotions not only reward hard work but also motivate others to step up and show their leadership qualities.
    - **Promote Based on Merit**: If they've demonstrated the necessary skills, promote them to managerial roles where they can expand their influence.

- **Reward Leadership Behavior**: Recognize leadership behaviors such as initiative, collaboration, and problem-solving, and offer incentives for such actions.
- **Ensure Smooth Transition**: Provide additional training and a clear transition plan to help them succeed in their new role.

Example: A retail business owner noticed that one of their floor staff consistently solved customer problems without supervision. They promoted her to Store Manager, and she eventually took over operations for multiple locations successfully.

Letting Go: Trusting Your Team to Lead

As your business grows, one of the most difficult but crucial challenges you will face is letting go of the control that's been central to your role as a solopreneur. But to scale your business, you must learn to trust your team.

Signs You're Ready to Step Back

You've worked hard to build your business, and now it's time to see it thrive without your constant presence. Here are signs that you're ready to take a step back and trust your team:

- Your EA and PC handle yours and your company's day-to-day tasks without constant input.
- Your managers make decisions confidently and handle challenges effectively.
- You spend more time on strategy, partnerships, and growth rather than operations.

How to Step Back Without Losing Control

Letting go of control doesn't mean disconnecting completely from your business—it means stepping back while still maintaining oversight and ensuring that the team is aligned with your vision.

1. Set Clear KPIs (Key Performance Indicators) for each team member.
2. Hold Weekly Leadership Meetings to stay updated without micromanaging.
3. Foster Open Communication so team members feel comfortable coming to you with important issues.
4. Celebrate Wins and recognize your leaders for their contributions.

Example: A business owner scheduled weekly leadership meetings with department heads, focusing on KPIs and growth strategies. This allowed them to step back from operations while staying informed.

Final Thoughts – From Operator to Leader

The transition from solopreneur to CEO isn't just about hiring people—it's about building systems, trusting your team, and focusing on growth.

- Delegate low-value tasks and focus on strategic growth.
- Build a second line of leadership that can run the business without you.
- Develop leaders from within and create a culture of ownership.
- Let go of control and trust your team to lead.

By mastering delegation and building a strong leadership team, you'll create a business that doesn't just rely on you—it thrives because of the systems and leaders you've put in place.

CHAPTER - 18

Revenue Allocation System (RAS): *Mastering Financial Control for SMEs*

One of the biggest struggles for SMEs in India is cash flow mismanagement. Many business owners make the mistake of mixing operational expenses, vendor payments, and profits in a single account, leading to financial confusion and difficulty in making payments on time.

To solve this, we introduce the Revenue Allocation System (RAS)—a structured way to manage cash flow, control expenses, and ensure financial discipline. This method ensures that every rupee you receive is allocated properly, making payments effortless and profit tracking crystal clear.

Revenue Allocation System

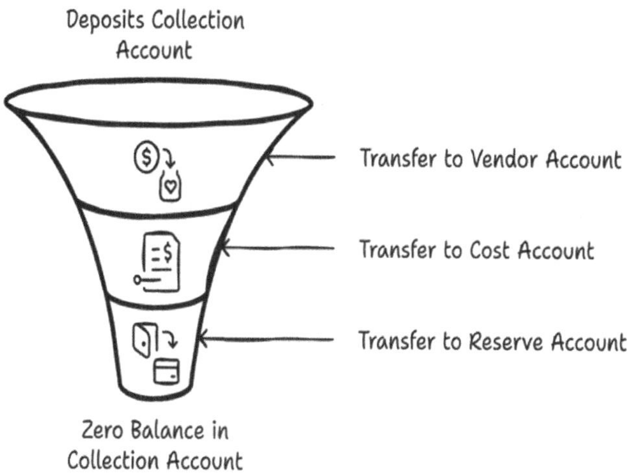

How RAS Works – The Four-Account System

To implement RAS, you will need four bank accounts—all of which your banker can open for you, even if you already have loan accounts and credit limits. Ask your bank to create these accounts as separate cost and profit centers.

Collection Account (Your Main Account)

- **Purpose:** This is where all your receivables, cash sales, and payments from customers will be deposited.
- **Type:** This can be your existing Current Account, Cash Credit (CC), or Overdraft (OD) Account.
- **Action:** At the end of each day, all money in this account must be distributed to the next three accounts based on your pre-decided percentage allocations.

Example: If you receive ₹1,00,000 in your Collection Account today, you will allocate this amount to the other accounts based on predefined cost percentages.

Vendor Account (New Current Account for Vendor Payments)

- **Purpose:** This account is strictly for paying vendors and suppliers.
- **How it Works:** From your Collection Account, transfer your Cost of Goods Sold (COGS) percentage to this account.
- **For Service Businesses:** If you are in the service industry, vendor payments could include software subscriptions, office supplies, or other operational consumables.

Example: If your gross profit margin is 20%, then your COGS is 80%. If you receive ₹1,00,000 in your Collection Account today, you will transfer ₹80,000 to this Vendor Account.

Cost Account (New Current Account for Fixed Costs)

- **Purpose:** This account is for salaries, rent, electricity, marketing, and other fixed expenses.
- **How it Works:** From your Collection Account, transfer the percentage needed for fixed costs.

Example: If fixed costs (salaries, rent, electricity) make up 12% of revenue, and you receive ₹1,00,000, transfer ₹12,000 to this account.

Reserve Account (EMI or New Current Account for Profits & Emergency Funds)

- **Purpose:** This account holds all remaining money after vendor payments and fixed costs—your real profit and reserves.
- **How it Works:** After transferring money to the Vendor and Cost Accounts, whatever is left in the Collection Account should go here.
- **Use Cases:** This can be used for loan EMIs, reinvestment, or emergency backup funds.

Example: If you received ₹1,00,000 today, and you've already allocated ₹80,000 to Vendor Account and ₹12,000 to Cost Account, the remaining ₹8,000 is your actual profit—this goes into the Reserve Account.

Daily Process – How to Execute RAS Effectively

Every day, before closing your business accounts, follow this simple end-of-day (EOD) process:

- **Step 1:** Check total deposits received in your Collection Account.
- **Step 2:** Transfer the appropriate percentages to Vendor Account and Cost Account.
- **Step 3:** Transfer the remaining balance to your Reserve Account.
- **Step 4:** Ensure your Collection Account is left with ₹0 at the end of the day.

Tip: Convert your Cash Credit (CC) / Overdraft (OD) accounts into long-term loans with a tenure of 10-15 years to ensure structured repayment. If your bank is unable to facilitate this, request a monthly dropline reduction of 1% on your CC/

OD limit. For example, if your CC/OD limit is ₹1 Crore, instruct your bank to reduce it by ₹1 lakh per month through standing instructions. This way, you will gradually repay your limit within 8 years, turning what once seemed impossible into a manageable and strategic debt reduction plan.

The Ultimate Benefit – Never Worry About Payments Again!

By diligently following this method, you will never struggle to make payments. Every rupee is accounted for, and you will always know exactly how much profit you are making.

This system, taught to me by my coach, is the most powerful cash flow management technique an SME can implement. Start using the Revenue Allocation System (RAS) today and take control of your business finances like never before!

CHAPTER - 19

Financial Discipline & Wealth Creation: *From Business Profits to Personal Wealth*

Many small and medium business owners focus on making money, but very few focus on keeping and growing it. The reality is that high revenue does not guarantee wealth—what matters is how well you manage, invest, and plan for the future.

Financial discipline is about more than just budgeting—it's about ensuring your business is profitable, paying the right taxes, and creating personal wealth from your business success.

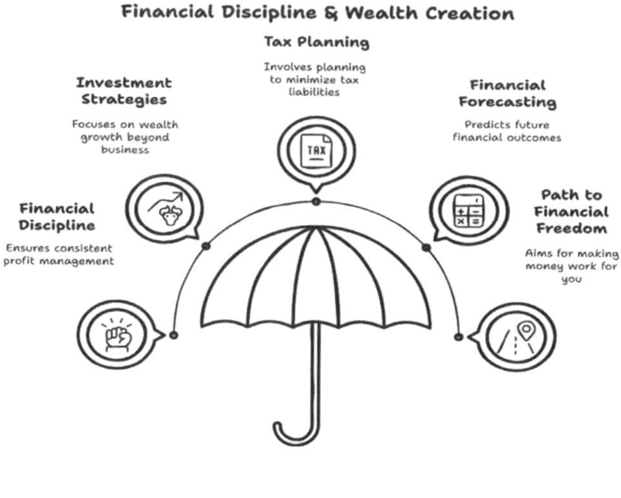

Financial Discipline & Long-Term Security for Business Owners

In this chapter, we'll cover;

- How to move beyond budgeting to long-term financial security
- The best investment strategies for business owners
- And how to plan your taxes and forecast your finances for sustainable growth.

Let's dive in!

1. Financial Discipline: Why Profitable Businesses Still Struggle

It's common to see businesses that generate high revenue but struggle with cash flow. Why? Because they lack financial discipline and treat business earnings as personal cash flow.

Common Financial Mistakes SMEs Make

- **Mixing personal and business finances:** Business owners withdraw money from the company without a clear system, leading to confusion and inefficiency.
- **Not tracking profitability properly:** Focusing only on revenue without understanding actual profit.
- **Ignoring tax planning:** Paying unnecessary penalties due to poor planning.
- **Spending everything instead of investing**: No funds are left for business expansion or personal wealth.

The Solution? Build a structured financial discipline plan.

2. Moving Beyond Budgeting: Managing Your Business Profits Wisely

Budgeting is only the first step in financial control. The next step is allocating your profits wisely.

Profit Allocation System (PAS): The 50-30-20 Rule

A simple way to manage business earnings effectively is using this structured allocation:

- **50% – Business Growth & Expansion**
  - Invest in marketing, hiring, and scaling operations.
  - Build an emergency fund for unexpected downturns.
- **30% – Personal Wealth & Investments**
  - Diversify earnings into investments like real estate, stocks, or mutual funds.
  - Save for long-term financial security (retirement, family security).
- **20% – Emergency**
  - Set aside funds for any emergency expenses.
  - Never get caught in any critical situation due to last-minute planning.

How to Implement PAS in Your Business

1. Firstly, open two more Current Accounts & one Savings Account (with Auto FD).

   a. 1st Current Account: Growth Account

   b. 2nd Current Account: Emergency Account

   c. Savings Account: Emergency Account (Auto FD)

2. At the end of each month, calculate your net profit or ask your finance manager to do so.

3. Transfer the respective amounts to separate accounts

   a. Growth Account: 50% of Net Profits

   b. Emergency Account: 20% of Net Profits

   c. Savings Account: 30% of Net Profits

4. Reinvest wisely—never drain all cash flow into expansion without saving for security.

   All these accounts are in addition to your 4 previously mentioned accounts.

   Example: If your monthly profit is ₹1,00,000, then:

   - ₹50,000 goes to business growth.
   - ₹30,000 is invested in personal assets.
   - ₹20,000 is reserved for emergencies.

3. **Investment Strategies: How to Grow Your Wealth Beyond Your Business**

   Most business owners keep all their wealth tied up in their business, which is risky. Diversifying your income is key to long-term wealth creation.

   Best Investment Options for Business Owners

   - **Stock Market & Mutual Funds** – Invest in stable, growth-oriented companies.
   - **Real Estate** – Buy commercial or rental properties for passive income.
   - **Fixed Deposits & Bonds** – Low-risk options for capital preservation.
   - **Gold & Precious Metals** – A hedge against inflation and market volatility.
   - **Startup Investments** – Invest in smaller businesses with high potential.

   Example: Instead of keeping ₹20,00,000 in a savings account, a business owner invests ₹10,00,000 in mutual funds, ₹5,00,000 in Gold, and ₹5,00,000 in fixed deposits—ensuring diversified income streams.

The Key Rule: Pay Yourself First

One of the most important rules in personal and business finance is "Pay Yourself First". Here's how it works:

- Every time your business makes a profit, set aside a fixed percentage for personal wealth building.
- Don't rely on your business as the only source of financial security.

4. **Tax Planning & Financial Forecasting: Stay Ahead, Not Behind**

Many business owners only think about taxes at the last minute, leading to unnecessary stress, penalties, and lost opportunities for savings. Proper tax planning can help you legally save money and optimize your profits.

Smart Tax Planning Strategies

1. **Use business expenses to lower taxable income** – Expenses like rent, travel, salaries, and software are tax-deductible. Keep thorough records to take advantage of these deductions.
2. **Invest in tax-saving instruments** – Instruments like ELSS, PPF, and NPS reduce your taxable income and give you long-term benefits.
3. **Opt for structured salary withdrawals** – Paying yourself a salary instead of random withdrawals helps optimize tax savings.
4. **Consult a tax expert** – A good accountant can **save you lakhs of rupees** per year by optimizing deductions.

Financial Forecasting: Planning for Growth & Stability

Financial forecasting ensures you always have enough cash flow for future expenses. Proper forecasting will help you plan for fluctuations in cash flow, so you're always prepared.

Steps to Financial Forecasting:

- **Project income & expenses**: Estimate your income and expenses for the next 6 to 12 months to have a clear picture of your financial future.
- **Identify potential financial risks**: By anticipating slow periods or unplanned expenses, you can create backup plans to ensure your business remains stable.
- **Set revenue goals & monitor progress**: Regularly track your performance to stay on target for your financial goals.

Example: A business owner forecasts their next 12 months of revenue & expenses, identifying slow months in advance and planning cash reserves accordingly.

5. The Path to Financial Freedom: Making Your Money Work for You

The ultimate goal of running a business isn't just making money—it's achieving financial independence.

1. Track your income, profits, and tax liabilities.
2. Allocate profits wisely using the 50-30-20 system.
3. Diversify into smart investments beyond your business.
4. Plan for taxes and forecast financial health in advance.

By following these principles, you won't just build a successful business—you'll build lasting wealth that secures your future.

CHAPTER - 20

Exit Strategy & Business Scaling: *Building a Sellable & Scalable Business*

Many business owners focus only on growing their business, but very few think about what happens next—whether they want to scale up, step back, or even sell the business one day.

A truly successful business is one that can run and grow without the owner's daily involvement. The key to achieving this is by building systems, automating processes, and making your business attractive to buyers or investors.

This chapter will help you understand:

- How to scale your business without working harder.
- How to prepare your business for an eventual exit or succession.
- How to make your business "sellable" so that investors see it as a valuable asset.

Why Every Business Needs an Exit Plan

Even if you love what you do, you won't always want to work in your business forever. Having an exit strategy doesn't mean you have to sell today—it just means that if an opportunity arises, you will be prepared.

Reasons Business Owners Consider an Exit:

- **Retirement or Lifestyle Change**: You may eventually want to step back from daily operations and enjoy the fruits of your labor.
- **Scaling Up or Getting Investors**: A well-structured business is more attractive to investors.
- **Selling the Business for a High Valuation**: A business with systems in place can command a higher sale price.
- **Passing It to the Next Generation**: Ensuring your children or successors inherit a well-run company.

Without an exit plan, many SME owners end up **stuck in their business forever**, unable to step away without things falling apart.

The Solution? Build a Business That Can Function Without You.

The 3-Step Framework for Scaling Without Chaos

Scaling a business isn't about working harder—it's about creating systems, hiring the right people, and automating processes so that the business can grow on its own.

Step 1: Systemize & Automate Operations

- Document all Standard Operating Procedures (SOPs).
- Implement Checklists (CLs) for daily operations.
- Use automation tools for finance and customer management.

Step 2: Build a Leadership Team to Take Over Key Roles

- Hire an Executive Assistant (EA) to manage your day-to-day.
- Appoint a Process Coordinator (PC) to enforce SOPs.

- Develop a second line of leadership (Operations Manager, Sales Head, Finance Manager) to take ownership of key business functions.

Step 3: Create a Scalable Business Model

- Identify new revenue streams (franchising, licensing, digital products, etc.).
- Optimize pricing and upselling to increase revenue without more effort.
- Focus on repeat business and customer retention strategies.

Example: A retail store owner introduced **franchise models** and delegated store operations to managers. By focusing on expanding the brand rather than being involved in daily tasks, the business grew from **one location to ten** in just five years. The owner only worked 8 hours a week, enjoying the benefits of a scalable business model.

Making Your Business Sellable – Even If You Don't Want to Sell Today

Even if you're not thinking about selling your business now, running it as if you will sell one day forces you to create a well-structured, valuable company.

What Makes a Business Attractive to Buyers & Investors?

Investors and buyers are looking for businesses that are not only profitable but structured in a way that allows them to continue growing without heavy involvement from the owner. Here's what makes a business attractive:

- **Strong Financials** – Predictable revenue, solid profit margins, and clean accounting records.

- **A Business That Doesn't Depend on the Owner** – Can it run smoothly without you?
- **Scalable Systems & SOPs** – Well-documented operations and automation.
- **Strong Brand & Market Position** – A loyal customer base and a unique value proposition.
- **Recurring Revenue Streams** – Subscription models, long-term contracts, or other passive income sources.

Example: A manufacturing business increased its valuation by 3X by simply implementing proper financial tracking, SOPs, and reducing dependency on the owner.

Exit Strategy Options – Choosing the Right Path

Once your business is structured in a way that makes it attractive to buyers or investors, you'll have several exit options:

Option 1: Selling the Business

- Sell to a competitor, investor, or private buyer.
- Get a business valuation and negotiate a deal.
- Use the funds for retirement or reinvesting in new ventures.

Option 2: Succession Planning – Passing It to the Next Generation

- Train family members or senior employees to take over.
- Transition ownership while keeping company stability.

Option 3: Hiring a CEO & Stepping Back

- Appoint a CEO or leadership team to run daily operations.
- Retain ownership while enjoying passive income.

Option 4: Mergers & Acquisitions

- Merge with a larger company for better financial growth.
- Get acquired by a bigger player in your industry.

Example: A business owner successfully transitioned from active management to earning passive income by hiring a CEO, freeing up time while still earning profits.

Final Thoughts – The Key to Long-Term Success

Achieving long-term success in your business—whether it's scaling or eventually exiting—requires intentional planning and effort. It's not something that happens overnight, but with the right strategy, you'll set yourself up for growth, financial security, and the freedom to make decisions about your future.

Key Takeaways:

- Start planning your exit early, even if you don't want to leave soon.
- Build systems so your business runs smoothly without you.
- Make your business attractive to investors by improving financials & operations.
- Explore multiple exit options—selling, succession, or stepping back.

A well-run business isn't just easier to manage—it's also more valuable. Whether you choose to sell, scale, or step back, having an exit strategy ensures you are always in control of your future.

Conclusion: *Your Journey to Business Freedom Begins Now*

You started this book looking for ways to automate, delegate, and dominate your business. Now, you have the exact roadmap to scale without stress, increase profits without effort, and create a business that works for you—rather than the other way around.

The difference between those who achieve exponential success and those who remain stuck is simple: Action.

It's time to take everything you've learned and start implementing. Your business is only as strong as the systems you build. So, take action today, and begin the process of building a business that serves your future ambitions.

Recap:
The Core Principles of This Book

1. **Time Mastery & Productivity**
   - **Golden Hour** – The first and most powerful hour of your day.
   - **Money Value of Time (MVT)** – Focus on high-value activities, not distractions.
   - **Deep Work & Scheduling** – Your calendar is your most powerful weapon.
   - **To-Do Lists & Prioritization** – The right work at the right time = rapid success.
2. **Delegation & Leadership**
   - **Hire an EA (Executive Assistant) & PC (Process Coordinator)** – The first steps to removing yourself from daily operations.
   - **Building a Leadership Team** – Your business must run without you.
   - **The Art of Delegation** – Stop being the bottleneck, start being the visionary.
3. **Automate & Systemize Everything**
   - **Checklists & SOPs** – The foundation of a stress-free business.

- **Automation Tools & Business Systems** – Leverage technology to run operations.
- **Revenue Allocation System (RAS)** – Financial clarity at all times.

4. **Financial Discipline & Scaling**
   - **Budgeting & Cost Cutting** – Profit is made in decisions, not just sales.
   - **Profit Myths & True Business Wealth** – Knowing your numbers is everything.
   - **Wealth Creation & Tax Planning** – Grow beyond just business income.
   - **Exit Strategy & Business Scaling** – Make your business sellable, scalable, and sustainable.

5. **Game-Changing Marketing**
   - **Stand Out & Be Unforgettable** – If you blend in, you disappear.
   - **Build a Community, Not Just Customers** – People want to be part of something bigger.
   - **Sell Stories, Not Just Products** – Emotion drives action, not logic.
   - **Leverage Permission-Based Marketing** – The best marketing is one that customers invite.

What's next? Implement!

Even if you start with just ONE system today, you're already ahead of 99% of entrepreneurs.

Stay Connected & Get Exclusive Business Automation Insights: *FREE*

Your journey doesn't end here. I want to help you implement these strategies, stay accountable, and continue scaling your business effortlessly.

Visit parasbambha.com and continue your automation journey.

Get FREE Regular Business Automation Tips & Strategies Straight to Your Phone!

- Exclusive insights not shared anywhere else.
- Direct Q&A opportunities & live webinars.
- Stay updated on the latest automation tools & business systems.

Here is the website link - https://parasbambha.com

This is your unfair advantage in business. Let's automate, delegate, and dominate—together.